Motivation

D1531191

MOTIVATION

A Harvard Business Review Paperback

Harvard Business Review paperback No. 90010

The *Harvard Business Review* articles in this collection are available individually. Discounts apply to quantity purchases. For information and ordering, contact Operations Department, Harvard Business School Publishing Division, Boston, MA 02163. Telephone: (617) 495-6192. Fax: (617) 495-6985.

© 1963, 1964, 1975, 1980, 1983, 1984, 1986, 1987, 1988, 1989, 1991 by the President and Fellows of Harvard College.

Editor's Note: Some articles included in this book may have been written before authors and editors began to take into consideration the role of women in management. We hope the archaic usage representing all managers as male does not detract from the usefulness of the collection.

All rights reserved. No part of this book may be reproduced, stored in a retrieval system, or transmitted, in any form or by any means, electronic, mechanical, photocopying, recording, or otherwise without the prior written permission of the copyright holder.
Printed in the United States of America.
93 92 91   5 4 3 2 1

Contents

What Motivation Is—and Is Not

One More Time:
How Do You Motivate Employees?
Frederick Herzberg
3

You don't motivate people with kicks (literal or figurative) or with inducement. An HBR classic and a runaway best seller.

Who Are Your Motivated Workers?
M. Scott Myers
15

Field research that confirms, extends, and deepens Herzberg's approach to motivation.

Real Work
Abraham Zaleznik
31

Workers would rather have a task leader than a social leader, a boss who is adept at substance rather than one skilled in politics.

Praise Reappraised
Richard E. Farson
39

Praise may be essentially manipulative and undermine authentic, self-sustaining motivation.

Motivating the Sales Force

Teamwork for Today's Selling
Frank V. Cespedes, Stephen X. Doyle, and Robert J. Freedman
47

The selling of industrial goods has become a lot more complicated; if selling goals have changed, motivation had better follow suit.

What Counts Most In Motivating Your Sales Force?
Stephen X. Doyle and Benson P. Shapiro
55

In the mix of factors motivating salespeople, the nature of the sales task has uncommon importance.

Make the Sales Task Clear
Benson P. Shapiro and Stephen X. Doyle
63

Ways of clearly specifying the sales task—even when that task is inherently vague.

Motivating Manufacturing Employees

Kratylus Automates His Urnworks
Tolly Kizilos
67

A fanciful Socratic dialogue that plumbs the definition of productivity and inquires how productivity can be enhanced.

**The Human Costs of
Manufacturing Reform**
Janice A. Klein
77

Ironically, the factory reforms that increase
worker responsibility for production can severely
constrain workers' autonomy, making them once
again mere extensions of a relentless system.

Doing Away with the Factory Blues
Donald N. Scobel
83

An eloquent but simple statement describing the
humanizing of a company's factories.

Pay and Performance

The Attack on Pay
Rosaabeth Moss Kanter
97

If you want to encourage results, pay the person,
not the position. But be prepared for big changes
in your organization.

Four Ways to Overpay Yourself Enough
Kenneth Mason
105

How do you change the corporate tendency to
pay executives like entrepreneurs when they
actually perform like bureaucrats?

**Top Executives Are Worth Every Nickel
They Get**
Kevin J. Murphy
111

The critics of excessive executive pay are wrong.
A hard look at compensation shows that it's
doing what it's designed to do.

**Compensation and Benefits for
Startup Companies**
*Joseph S. Tibbetts, Jr.
and Edmund T. Donovan*
119

A startup can't afford the compensation packages
of larger organizations, but even in this area,
there are advantages to being small.

What Motivation Is— and Is Not

One more time: How do you motivate employees?

HBR Classic

Frederick Herzberg

How many articles, books, speeches, and workshops have pleaded plaintively, "How do I get an employee to do what I want?"

The psychology of motivation is tremendously complex, and what has been unraveled with any degree of assurance is small indeed. But the dismal ratio of knowledge to speculation has not dampened the enthusiasm for new forms of snake oil that are constantly coming on the market, many of them with academic testimonials. Doubtless this article will have no depressing impact on the market for snake oil, but since the ideas expressed in it have been tested in many corporations and other organizations, it will help – I hope – to redress the imbalance in the aforementioned ratio.

'Motivating' with KITA

In lectures to industry on the problem, I have found that the audiences are anxious for quick and practical answers, so I will begin with a straightforward, practical formula for moving people.

To mark the 65th birthday of the Harvard Business Review, *it's appropriate to republish as a "Classic" one of its landmark articles. Frederick Herzberg's contribution has sold more than 1.2 million reprints since its publication in the January-February 1968 issue. By some 300,000 copies over the runner-up, that is the largest sale of any of the thousands of articles that have ever appeared between HBR's covers.*

Frederick Herzberg, Distinguished Professor of Management at the University of Utah, was head of the department of psychology at Case Western Reserve University when he wrote this article. His writings include the book Work and the Nature of Man *(World, 1966).*

What is the simplest, surest, and most direct way of getting someone to do something? Ask? But if the person responds that he or she does not want to do it, then that calls for psychological consultation to determine the reason for such obstinacy. Tell the person? The response shows that he or she does not understand you, and now an expert in communication methods has to be brought in to show you how to get through. Give the person a monetary incentive? I do not need to remind the reader of the complexity and difficulty involved in setting up and administering an incentive system. Show the person? This means a costly training program. We need a simple way.

Every audience contains the "direct action" manager who shouts, "Kick the person!" And this type of manager is right. The surest and least circumlocuted way of getting someone to do something is to administer a kick in the pants – to give what might be called the KITA.

There are various forms of KITA, and here are some of them:

Negative physical KITA. This is a literal application of the term and was frequently used in the past. It has, however, three major drawbacks: (1) it is inelegant; (2) it contradicts the precious image of benevolence that most organizations cherish; and (3) since it is a physical attack, it directly stimulates the autonomic nervous system, and this often results in negative feedback – the employee may just kick you in return. These factors give rise to certain taboos against negative physical KITA.

In uncovering infinite sources of psychological vulnerabilities and the appropriate methods to play tunes on them, psychologists have come to the rescue of those who are no longer permitted to use negative physical KITA. "He took my rug away"; "I wonder what she meant by that"; "The boss is always going around me" – these symptomatic expressions of ego sores that have been rubbed raw are the result of application of:

Negative psychological KITA. This has several advantages over negative physical KITA. First, the cruelty is not visible; the bleeding is internal and comes much later. Second, since it affects the higher cortical centers of the brain with its inhibitory powers, it reduces the possibility of physical backlash. Third, since the number of psychological pains that a person can feel is almost infinite, the direction and site possibilities of the KITA are increased many times. Fourth, the person administering the kick can manage to be above it all and let the system accomplish the dirty work. Fifth, those who practice it receive some ego satisfaction (one-upmanship), whereas they would find drawing blood abhorrent. Finally, if the employee does complain, he or she can always be accused of being paranoid; there is no tangible evidence of an actual attack.

Now, what does negative KITA accomplish? If I kick you in the rear (physically or psychologically), who is motivated? *I* am motivated; *you* move! Negative KITA does not lead to motivation, but to movement. So:

Positive KITA. Let us consider motivation. If I say to you, "Do this for me or the company, and in return I will give you a reward, an incentive, more status, a promotion, all the quid pro quos that exist in the industrial organization," am I motivating you? The overwhelming opinion I receive from management people is, "Yes, this is motivation."

I have a year-old Schnauzer. When it was a small puppy and I wanted it to move, I kicked it in the rear and it moved. Now that I have finished its obedience training, I hold up a dog biscuit when I want the Schnauzer to move. In this instance, who is motivated—I or the dog? The dog wants the biscuit, but it is I who want it to move. Again, I am the one who is motivated, and the dog is the one who moves. In this instance all I did was apply KITA frontally; I exerted a pull instead of a push. When industry wishes to use such positive KITAs, it has available an incredible number and variety of dog biscuits (jelly beans for humans) to wave in front of employees to get them to jump.

Why is it that managerial audiences are quick to see that negative KITA is *not* motivation, while they are almost unanimous in their judgment that positive KITA *is* motivation. It is because negative KITA is rape, and positive KITA is seduction. But it is infinitely worse to be seduced than to be raped; the latter is an unfortunate occurrence, while the former signifies that you were a party to your own downfall. This is why positive KITA is so popular: it is a tradition; it is the American way. The organization does not have to kick you; you kick yourself.

Myths about motivation

Why is KITA not motivation? If I kick my dog (from the front or the back), he will move. And when I want him to move again, what must I do? I must kick him again. Similarly, I can charge a person's battery, and then recharge it, and recharge it again. But it is only when one has a generator of one's own that we can talk about motivation. One then needs no outside stimulation. One *wants* to do it.

With this in mind, we can review some positive KITA personnel practices that were developed as attempts to instill "motivation":

1 **Reducing time spent at work.** This represents a marvelous way of motivating people to work—getting them off the job! We have reduced (formally and informally) the time spent on the job over the last 50 or 60 years until we are finally on the way to the "6½-day weekend." An interesting variant of this approach is the development of off-hour recreation programs. The philosophy here seems to be that those who play together, work together. The fact is that motivated people seek more hours of work, not fewer.

2 **Spiraling wages.** Have these motivated people? Yes, to seek the next wage increase. Some medievalists still can be heard to say that a good depression will get employees moving. They feel that if rising wages don't or won't do the job, reducing them will.

3 **Fringe benefits.** Industry has outdone the most welfare-minded of welfare states in dispensing cradle-to-the-grave succor. One company I know of had an informal "fringe benefit of the month club" going for a while. The cost of fringe benefits in this country has reached approximately 25% of the wage dollar, and we still cry for motivation.

People spend less time working for more money and more security than ever before, and the trend cannot be reversed. These benefits are no longer rewards; they are rights. A 6-day week is inhuman, a 10-hour day is exploitation, extended medical coverage is a basic decency, and stock options are the salvation of American initiative. Unless the ante is continuously raised, the psychological reaction of employees is that the company is turning back the clock.

When industry began to realize that both the economic nerve and the lazy nerve of their employees had insatiable appetites, it started to listen to the behavioral scientists who, more out of a humanist tradition than from scientific study, criticized management for not knowing how to deal with people. The next KITA easily followed.

4   **Human relations training.** Over 30 years of teaching and, in many instances, of practicing psychological approaches to handling people have resulted in costly human relations programs and, in the end, the same question: How do you motivate workers? Here, too, escalations have taken place. Thirty years ago it was necessary to request, "Please don't spit on the floor." Today the same admonition requires three "pleases" before the employee feels that a superior has demonstrated the psychologically proper attitude.

The failure of human relations training to produce motivation led to the conclusion that supervisors or managers themselves were not psychologically true to themselves in their practice of interpersonal decency. So an advanced form of human relations KITA, sensitivity training, was unfolded.

5   **Sensitivity training.** Do you really, really understand yourself? Do you really, really, really trust other people? Do you really, really, really, really cooperate? The failure of sensitivity training is now being explained, by those who have become opportunistic exploiters of the technique, as a failure to really (five times) conduct proper sensitivity training courses.

With the realization that there are only temporary gains from comfort and economic and interpersonal KITA, personnel managers concluded that the fault lay not in what they were doing, but in the employee's failure to appreciate what they were doing. This opened up the field of communications, a whole new area of "scientifically" sanctioned KITA.

6   **Communications.** The professor of communications was invited to join the faculty of management training programs and help in making employees understand what management was doing for them. House organs, briefing sessions, supervisory instruction on the importance of communication, and all sorts of propaganda have proliferated until today there is even an International Council of Industrial Editors. But no motivation resulted, and the obvious thought occurred that perhaps management was not hearing what the employees were saying. That led to the next KITA.

7   **Two-way communication.** Management ordered morale surveys, suggestion plans, and group participation programs. Then both employees and management were communicating and listening to each other more than ever, but without much improvement in motivation.

The behavioral scientists began to take another look at their conceptions and their data, and they took human relations one step further. A glimmer of truth was beginning to show through in the writings of the so-called higher-order-need psychologists. People, so they said, want to actualize themselves. Unfortunately, the "actualizing" psychologists got mixed up with the human relations psychologists, and a new KITA emerged.

8   **Job participation.** Though it may not have been the theoretical intention, job participation often became a "give them the big picture" approach. For example, if a man is tightening 10,000 nuts a day on an assembly line with a torque wrench, tell him he is building a Chevrolet. Another approach had the goal of giving employees a "feeling" that they are determining, in some measure, what they do on the job. The goal was to provide a *sense* of achievement rather than a substantive achievement in the task. Real achievement, of course, requires a task that makes it possible.

But still there was no motivation. This led to the inevitable conclusion that the employees must be sick, and therefore to the next KITA.

9   **Employee counseling.** The initial use of this form of KITA in a systematic fashion can be credited to the Hawthorne experiment of the Western Electric Company during the early 1930s. At that time, it was found that the employees harbored irrational feelings that were interfering with the rational operation of the factory. Counseling in this instance was a means of letting the employees unburden themselves by talking to someone about their problems. Although the counseling techniques were primitive, the program was large indeed.

The counseling approach suffered as a result of experiences during World War II, when the programs themselves were found to be interfering with the operation of the organizations; the counselors had forgotten their role of benevolent listeners and were attempting to do something about the the problems that they heard about. Psychological counseling, however, has managed to survive the negative impact of World War II experiences and today is beginning to flourish with renewed sophistication. But, alas, many of these programs, like all the others, do not seem to have lessened the pressure of demands to find out how to motivate workers.

Since KITA results only in short-term movement, it is safe to predict that the cost of these programs will increase steadily and new varieties will be developed as old positive KITAs reach their satiation points.

Hygiene vs. motivators

Let me rephrase the perennial question this way: How do you install a generator in an employ-

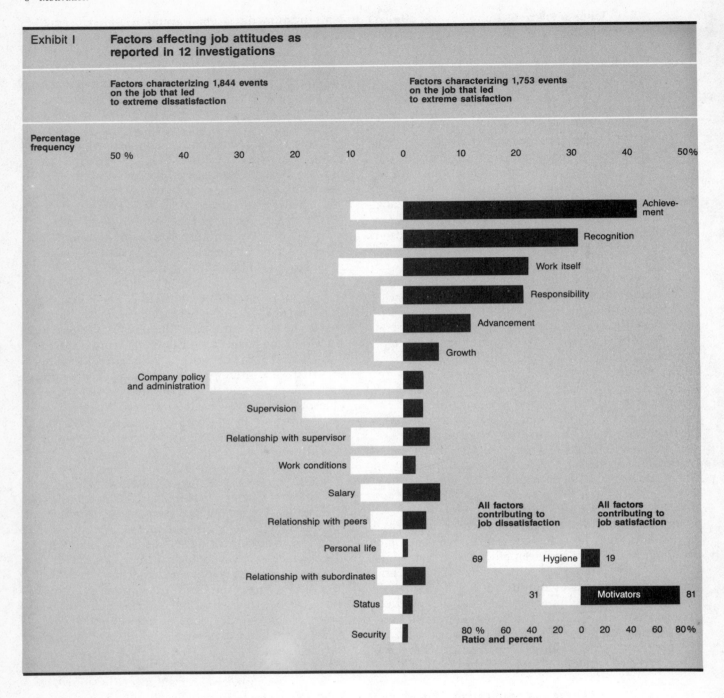

| Exhibit I | Factors affecting job attitudes as reported in 12 investigations |

Factors characterizing 1,844 events on the job that led to extreme dissatisfaction

Factors characterizing 1,753 events on the job that led to extreme satisfaction

Percentage frequency

50 %   40   30   20   10   0   10   20   30   40   50%

Achievement
Recognition
Work itself
Responsibility
Advancement
Growth
Company policy and administration
Supervision
Relationship with supervisor
Work conditions
Salary
Relationship with peers
Personal life
Relationship with subordinates
Status
Security

All factors contributing to job dissatisfaction

All factors contributing to job satisfaction

69   Hygiene   19

31   Motivators   81

80 %   60   40   20   0   20   40   60   80%
Ratio and percent

ee? A brief review of my motivation-hygiene theory of job attitudes is required before theoretical and practical suggestions can be offered. The theory was first drawn from an examination of events in the lives of engineers and accountants. At least 16 other investigations, using a wide variety of populations (including some in the Communist countries), have since been completed, making the original research one of the most replicated studies in the field of job attitudes.

The findings of these studies, along with corroboration from many other investigations using different procedures, suggest that the factors in-

volved in producing job satisfaction (and motivation) are separate and distinct from the factors that lead to job dissatisfaction. Since separate factors need to be considered, depending on whether job satisfaction or job dissatisfaction is being examined, it follows that these two feelings are not opposites of each other. The opposite of job satisfaction is not job dissatisfaction but, rather, *no* job satisfaction; and similarly, the opposite of job dissatisfaction is not job satisfaction, but *no* job dissatisfaction.

Stating the concept presents a problem in semantics, for we normally think of satisfaction and dissatisfaction as opposites—i.e., what is not satisfying must be dissatisfying, and vice versa. But when it comes to understanding the behavior of people in their jobs, more than a play on words is involved.

Two different needs of human beings are involved here. One set of needs can be thought of as stemming from humankind's animal nature—the built-in drive to avoid pain from the environment, plus all the learned drives that become conditioned to the basic biological needs. For example, hunger, a basic biological drive, makes it necessary to earn money, and then money becomes a specific drive. The other set of needs relates to that unique human characteristic, the ability to achieve and, through achievement, to experience psychological growth. The stimuli for the growth needs are tasks that induce growth; in the industrial setting, they are the job content. *Contrariwise*, the stimuli inducing pain-avoidance behavior are found in the job environment.

The growth or *motivator* factors that are intrinsic to the job are: achievement, recognition for achievement, the work itself, responsibility, and growth or advancement. The dissatisfaction-avoidance or *hygiene* (KITA) factors that are extrinsic to the job include: company policy and administration, supervision, interpersonal relationships, working conditions, salary, status, and security.

A composite of the factors that are involved in causing job satisfaction and job dissatisfaction, drawn from samples of 1,685 employees, is shown in *Exhibit I*. The results indicate that motivators were the primary cause of satisfaction, and hygiene factors the primary cause of unhappiness on the job. The employees, studied in 12 different investigations, included lower level supervisors, professional women, agricultural administrators, men about to retire from management positions, hospital maintenance personnel, manufacturing supervisors, nurses, food handlers, military officers, engineers, scientists, housekeepers, teachers, technicians, female assemblers, accountants, Finnish foremen, and Hungarian engineers.

They were asked what job events had occurred in their work that had led to extreme satisfaction or extreme dissatisfaction on their part. Their responses are broken down in the exhibit into percentages of total "positive" job events and of total "negative" job events. (The figures total more than 100% on both the "hygiene" and "motivators" sides because often at least two factors can be attributed to a single event; advancement, for instance, often accompanies assumption of responsibility.)

To illustrate, a typical response involving achievement that had a negative effect for the employee was, "I was unhappy because I didn't do the job successfully." A typical response in the small number of positive job events in the company policy and administration grouping was, "I was happy because the company reorganized the section so that I didn't report any longer to the guy I didn't get along with."

As the lower right-hand part of the exhibit shows, of all the factors contributing to job satisfaction, 81% were motivators. And of all the factors contributing to the employees' dissatisfaction over their work, 69% involved hygiene elements.

Eternal triangle

There are three general philosophies of personnel management. The first is based on organizational theory, the second on industrial engineering, and the third on behavioral science.

Organizational theorists believe that human needs are either so irrational or so varied and adjustable to specific situations that the major function of personnel management is to be as pragmatic as the occasion demands. If jobs are organized in a proper manner, they reason, the result will be the most efficient job structure, and the most favorable job attitudes will follow as a matter of course.

Industrial engineers hold that humankind is mechanistically oriented and economically motivated and that human needs are best met by attuning the individual to the most efficient work process. The goal of personnel management therefore should be to concoct the most appropriate incentive system and to design the specific working conditions in a way that facilitates the most efficient use of the human machine. By structuring jobs in a manner that leads to the most efficient operation, engineers believe that they can obtain the optimal organization of work and the proper work attitudes.

Behavioral scientists focus on group sentiments, attitudes of individual employees, and the organization's social and psychological climate. This persuasion emphasizes one or more of the various hygiene and motivator needs. Its approach to personnel management is generally to emphasize some form of human relations education, in the hope of instilling healthy employee attitudes and an organizational climate that is considered to be felicitous to human values. The belief is that proper attitudes will lead to efficient job and organizational structure.

There is always a lively debate about the overall effectiveness of the approaches of organizational theorists and industrial engineers. Manifestly both have achieved much. But the nagging question for behavorial scientists has been: What is the cost in human problems that eventually cause more expense to the organization—for instance, turnover, absenteeism, errors, violation of safety rules, strikes, restriction of output, higher wages, and greater fringe benefits? On the other hand, behavioral scientists are hard put to document much manifest improvement in personnel management, using their approach.

The three philosophies can be depicted as a triangle, as is done in *Exhibit II*, with each persuasion claiming the apex angle. The motivation-hygiene theory claims the same angle as industrial engineering, but for opposite goals. Rather than rationalizing the work to increase efficiency, the theory suggests that work be *enriched* to bring about effective utilization of personnel. Such a systematic attempt to motivate employees by manipulating the motivator factors is just beginning.

The term *job enrichment* describes this embryonic movement. An older term, job enlargement, should be avoided because it is associated with past failures stemming from a misunderstanding of the problem. Job enrichment provides the opportunity for the employee's psychological growth, while job enlargement merely makes a job structurally bigger. Since scientific job enrichment is very new, this article only suggests the principles and practical steps that have recently emerged from several successful experiments in industry.

Job loading

In attempting to enrich certain jobs, management often reduces the personal contribution of employees rather than giving them opportunities for growth in their accustomed jobs. Such endeavors, which I shall call horizontal job loading (as opposed to vertical loading, or providing motivator factors), have been the problem of earlier job enlargement programs. Job loading merely enlarges the meaninglessness of the job. Some examples of this approach, and their effect, are:

☐ Challenging the employee by increasing the amount of production expected. If each tightens 10,000 bolts a day, see if each can tighten 20,000 bolts a day. The arithmetic involved shows that multiplying zero by zero still equals zero.

☐ Adding another meaningless task to the existing one, usually some routine clerical activity. The arithmetic here is adding zero to zero.

☐ Rotating the assignments of a number of jobs that need to be enriched. This means washing dishes for a while, then washing silverware. The arithmetic is substituting one zero for another zero.

☐ Removing the most difficult parts of the assignment in order to free the worker to accomplish more of the less challenging assignments. This traditional industrial engineering approach amounts to subtraction in the hope of accomplishing addition.

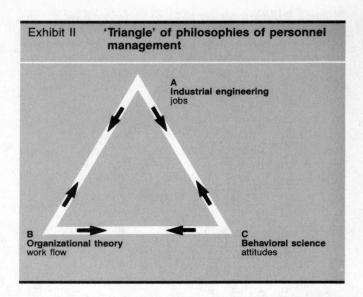

| Exhibit II | 'Triangle' of philosophies of personnel management |

A
Industrial engineering
jobs

B
Organizational theory
work flow

C
Behavioral science
attitudes

| Exhibit III | Principles of vertical job loading |

Principle	Motivators involved
A Removing some controls while retaining accountability	Responsibility and personal achievement
B Increasing the accountability of individuals for own work	Responsibility and recognition
C Giving a person a complete natural unit of work (module, division, area, and so on)	Responsibility, achievement, and recognition
D Granting additional authority to employees in their activity; job freedom	Responsibility, achievement, and recognition
E Making periodic reports directly available to the workers themselves rather than to supervisors	Internal recognition
F Introducing new and more difficult tasks not previously handled	Growth and learning
G Assigning individuals specific or specialized tasks, enabling them to become experts	Responsibility, growth, and advancement

These are common forms of horizontal loading that frequently come up in preliminary brainstorming sessions of job enrichment. The principles of vertical loading have not all been worked out as yet, and they remain rather general, but I have furnished seven useful starting points for consideration in *Exhibit III*.

A successful application

An example from a highly successful job enrichment experiment can illustrate the distinction between horizontal and vertical loading of a job. The subjects of this study were the stockholder correspondents employed by a very large corporation. Seemingly, the task required of these carefully selected and highly trained correspondents was quite complex and challenging. But almost all indexes of performance and job attitudes were low, and exit interviewing confirmed that the challenge of the job existed merely as words.

A job enrichment project was initiated in the form of an experiment with one group, designated as an achieving unit, having its job enriched by the principles described in *Exhibit III*. A control group continued to do its job in the traditional way. (There were also two "uncommitted" groups of correspondents formed to measure the so-called Hawthorne Effect— that is, to gauge whether productivity and attitudes toward the job changed artificially merely because employees sensed that the company was paying more attention to them in doing something different or novel. The results for these groups were substantially the same as for the control group, and for the sake of simplicity I do not deal with them in this summary.) No changes in hygiene were introduced for either group other than those that would have been made anyway, such as normal pay increases.

The changes for the achieving unit were introduced in the first two months, averaging one per week of the seven motivators listed in *Exhibit III*. At the end of six months the members of the achieving unit were found to be outperforming their counterparts in the control group, and in addition indicated a marked increase in their liking for their jobs. Other results showed that the achieving group had lower absenteeism and, subsequently, a much higher rate of promotion.

Exhibit IV illustrates the changes in performance, measured in February and March, before the study period began, and at the end of each month of the study period. The shareholder service index represents quality of letters, including accuracy of information, and speed of response to stockholders' letters of inquiry. The index of a current month was averaged into the average of the two prior months, which means that improvement was harder to obtain if the indexes of the previous months were low. The "achievers" were performing less well before the six-month period started, and their performance service index continued to decline after the introduction of the motivators, evidently because of uncertainty after their newly granted responsibilities. In the third month, however, performance improved, and soon the members of this group had reached a high level of accomplishment.

Exhibit V shows the two groups' attitudes toward their job, measured at the end of March, just before the first motivator was introduced, and again at the end of September. The correspondents were asked 16 questions, all involving motivation. A typical one was, "As you see it, how many opportunities do you feel that you have in your job for making worthwhile contributions?" The answers were scaled

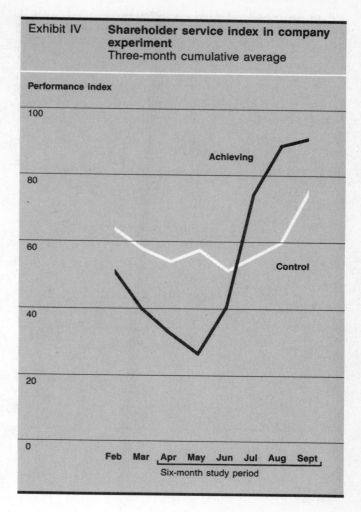

Exhibit IV   **Shareholder service index in company experiment**
Three-month cumulative average

Performance index

from 1 to 5, with 80 as the maximum possible score. The achievers became much more positive about their job, while the attitude of the control unit remained about the same (the drop is not statistically significant).

How was the job of these correspondents restructured? *Exhibit VI* lists the suggestions made that were deemed to be horizontal loading, and the actual vertical loading changes that were incorporated in the job of the achieving unit. The capital letters under "Principle" after "Vertical loading" refer to the corresponding letters in *Exhibit III*. The reader will note that the rejected forms of horizontal loading correspond closely to the list of common manifestations I mentioned earlier.

Steps for job enrichment

Now that the motivator idea has been described in practice, here are the steps that managers

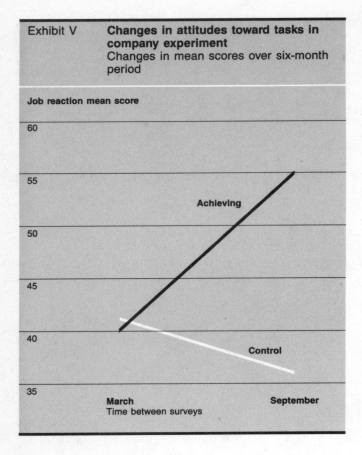

Exhibit V   **Changes in attitudes toward tasks in company experiment**
Changes in mean scores over six-month period

Job reaction mean score

60

55

Achieving

50

45

40

Control

35

March   September
Time between surveys

should take in instituting the principle with their employees:

1   Select those jobs in which (a) the investment in industrial engineering does not make changes too costly, (b) attitudes are poor, (c) hygiene is becoming very costly, and (d) motivation will make a difference in performance.

2   Approach these jobs with the conviction that they can be changed. Years of tradition have led managers to believe that the content of the jobs is sacrosanct and the only scope of action that they have is in ways of stimulating people.

3   Brainstorm a list of changes that may enrich the jobs, without concern for their practicality.

4   Screen the list to eliminate suggestions that involve hygiene, rather than actual motivation.

5   Screen the list for generalities, such as "give them more responsibility," that are rarely followed in practice. This might seem obvious, but the motivator words have never left industry; the substance has just been rationalized and organized out. Words like "responsibility," "growth," "achievement," and "challenge," for example, have been elevated to the lyrics of the patriotic anthem for all organizations. It is the old problem typified by the pledge of allegiance to the flag being more important than contributions to the country—of following the form, rather than the substance.

6   Screen the list to eliminate any *horizontal* loading suggestions.

7   Avoid direct participation by the employees whose jobs are to be enriched. Ideas they have expressed previously certainly constitute a valuable source for recommended changes, but their direct involvement contaminates the process with human relations *hygiene* and, more specifically, gives them only a *sense* of making a contribution. The job is to be changed, and it is the content that will produce the motivation, not attitudes about being involved or the challenge inherent in setting up a job. That process will be over shortly, and it is what the employees will be doing from then on that will determine their motivation. A sense of participation will result only in short-term movement.

8   In the initial attempts at job enrichment, set up a controlled experiment. At least two equivalent groups should be chosen, one an experimental unit in which the motivators are systematically introduced over a period of time, and the other one a control group in which no changes are made. For both groups, hygiene should be allowed to follow its natural course for the duration of the experiment. Pre- and post-installation tests of performance and job attitudes are necessary to evaluate the effectiveness of the job enrichment program. The attitude test must be limited to motivator items in order to divorce employees' views of the jobs they are given from all the surrounding hygiene feelings that they might have.

9   Be prepared for a drop in performance in the experimental group the first few weeks. The changeover to a new job may lead to a temporary reduction in efficiency.

10   Expect your first-line supervisors to experience some anxiety and hostility over the changes you are making. The anxiety comes from their fear that the changes will result in poorer performance for their unit. Hostility will arise when the employees start assuming what the supervisors regard as their own responsibility for performance. The supervisor without checking duties to perform may then be left with little to do.

After successful experiment, however, the supervisors usually discover the supervisory and managerial functions they have neglected, or which were never theirs because all their time was given over to checking the work of their subordinates. For example, in the R&D division of one large chemical company I know of, the supervisors of the laboratory assistants were theoretically responsible for their training and evaluation. These functions, however, had come to be performed in a routine, unsubstantial fashion. After the job enrichment program, during which the supervi-

Exhibit VI Enlargement vs. enrichment of correspondents' tasks in company experiment

Horizontal loading suggestions rejected	Vertical loading suggestions adopted	Principle
Firm quotas could be set for letters to be answered each day, using a rate which would be hard to reach.	Subject matter experts were appointed within each unit for other members of the unit to consult with before seeking supervisory help. (The supervisor had been answering all specialized and difficult questions.)	G
The secretaries could type the letters themselves, as well as compose them, or take on any other clerical functions.	Correspondents signed their own names on letters. (The supervisor had been signing all letters.)	B
All difficult or complex inquiries could be channeled to a few secretaries so that the remainder could achieve high rates of output. These jobs could be exchanged from time to time.	The work of the more experienced correspondents was proofread less frequently by supervisors and was done at the correspondents' desks, dropping verification from 100% to 10%. (Previously, all correspondents' letters had been checked by the supervisor.)	A
The secretaries could be rotated through units handling different customers, and then sent back to their own units.	Production was discussed, but only in terms such as "a full day's work is expected." As time went on, this was no longer mentioned. (Before, the group had been constantly reminded of the number of letters that needed to be answered.)	D
	Outgoing mail went directly to the mailroom without going over supervisors' desks. (The letters had always been routed through the supervisors.)	A
	Correspondents were encouraged to answer letters in a more personalized way. (Reliance on the form-letter approach had been standard practice.)	C
	Each correspondent was held personally responsible for the quality and accuracy of letters. (This responsibility had been the province of the supervisor and the verifier.)	B, E

sors were not merely passive observers of the assistants' performance, the supervisors actually were devoting their time to reviewing performance and administering thorough training.

What has been called an employee-centered style of supervision will come about not through education of supervisors, but by changing the jobs that they do.

Concluding note

Job enrichment will not be a one-time proposition, but a continuous management function. The initial changes should last for a very long period of time. There are a number of reasons for this:

☐ The changes should bring the job up to the level of challenge commensurate with the skill that was hired.

☐ Those who have still more ability eventually will be able to demonstrate it better and win promotion to higher level jobs.

☐ The very nature of motivators, as opposed to hygiene factors, is that they have a much longer term effect on employees' attitudes. Perhaps the job will have to be enriched again, but this will not occur as frequently as the need for hygiene.

Not all jobs can be enriched, nor do all jobs need to be enriched. If only a small percentage of the time and money that is now devoted to hygiene, however, were given to job enrichment efforts, the return in human satisfaction and economic gain would be one of the largest dividends that industry and society have ever reaped through their efforts at better personnel management.

The argument for job enrichment can be summed up quite simply: if you have employees on a job, use them. If you can't use them on the job, get rid of them, either via automation or by selecting someone with lesser ability. If you can't use them and you can't get rid of them, you will have a motivation problem.

[See Retrospective Commentary on following page]

Retrospective commentary

I wrote this article at the height of the attention on improving employee performance through various (contrived) psychological approaches to human relations. I tried to redress industrial social scientists' overconcern about how to treat workers to the neglect of how to design the work itself.

The first part of the article distinguishes between motivation and movement, a distinction that most writing on motivation misses. Movement is a function of fear of punishment or failure to get extrinsic rewards. It is the typical procedure used in animal training and its counterpart, behavioral modification techniques for humans. Motivation is a function of growth from getting intrinsic rewards out of interesting and challenging work.

While the immediate behavioral results from movement and motivation appear alike, their dynamics, which produce vastly different long-term consequences, are different. Movement requires constant reinforcement and stresses short-term results. To get a reaction, management must constantly enhance the extrinsic rewards for movement. If I get a bonus of $1,000 one

year and $500 the next, I am getting extra rewards both years, but psychologically I have taken a $500 salary cut.

Motivation is based on growth needs. It is an internal engine, and its benefits show up over a long period of time. Because the ultimate reward in motivation is personal growth, people don't need to be rewarded incrementally. I write a book—a big accomplishment. Then I write an article—a lesser accomplishment, but nevertheless an addition to my personal growth.

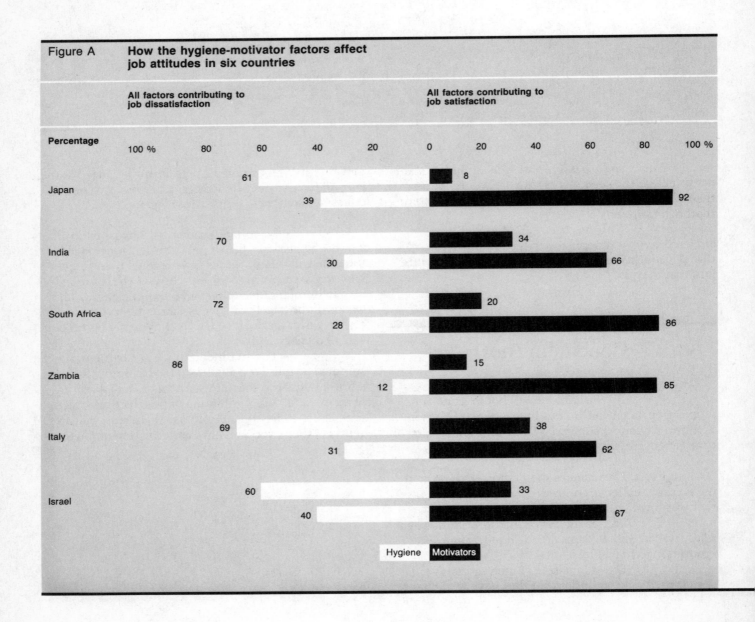

Figure A   How the hygiene-motivator factors affect job attitudes in six countries

For this article, I invented the acronym KITA (kick in the ass) to describe the movement technique. The inelegance of the term offended those who consider good treatment a motivating strategy, regardless of the nature of the work itself. In this plain language I tried to spotlight the animal approach to dealing with human beings that characterizes so much of our behavioral science intervention.

The article's popularity stems in great part from readers' recognition that KITA underlies the assumed benevolence of personnel practices. If I were writing "One More Time" in 1987, I would emphasize the important, positive role of organizational behaviorists more than I did in 1968. We can certainly learn to get along better on the job. Reduced workplace tension through congenial relations is a necessary ingredient of a pleasant environment.

The second part of the article describes my motivation-hygiene theory. It suggests that environmental factors (hygienes) can at best create no dissatisfaction on the job, and their absence creates dissatisfaction. In contrast,

Figure B   Sensory ingredients of job enrichment

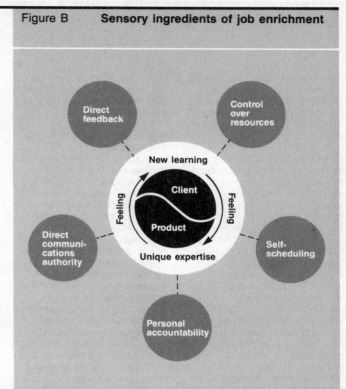

Figure C   Client relationships in an Air Force function

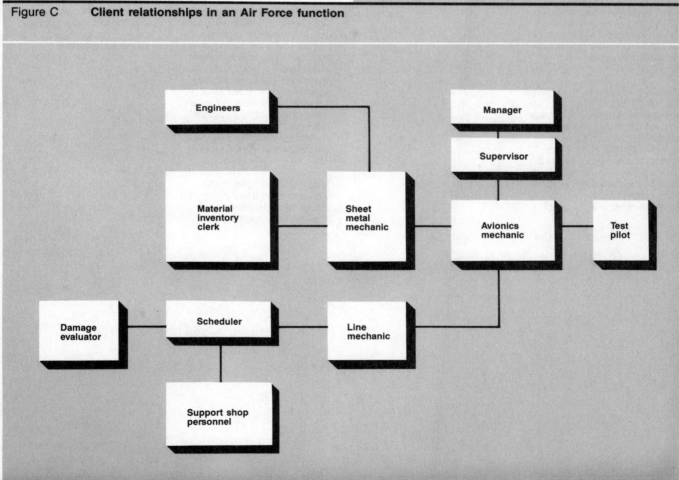

what makes people happy on the job and motivates them are the job content factors (motivators). The controversy surrounding these concepts continues to this day.

While the original 12 studies were mostly American (they also included Finnish supervisors and Hungarian engineers), the results have been replicated throughout the world. A sampling of recent foreign investigations, which the reader can compare with the first American studies detailed in *Exhibit I* in "One More Time," appears in *Figure A*. The similarity of the profiles is worth noting.

The 1970s was the decade of job enrichment (discussed in the third part of the article), sometimes called job design or redesign by opponents of the motivation-hygiene theory. Since the first trial-and-error studies at AT&T, experience has produced refinements of the procedures for job enrichment and the goals for achieving it. I like to illustrate them in the wheel shown in *Figure B*.

This diagram reflects my conviction that the present-day abstraction of work has shut out feelings from the job content. Finance, for example, has become the focus of attention in most businesses, and nothing is more abstract and devoid of feeling. Part of the blame can be laid to electronic communication, which promotes detachment and ab-

straction. Job enrichment grows out of knowing your product and your client with feeling, not just intellectually.

With reference to the motivator ingredients discussed in the 1968 article, "recognition for achievement" translates into "direct feedback" in *Figure B*. The wheel in *Figure B* shows this feedback to come chiefly from the client and product of the work itself, not from the supervisor (except in the case of new hires). The motivator factor "responsibility" translates into a number of ingredients: self-scheduling, authority to communicate, control of resources, and accountability. Finally, the motivator factors "advancement" and "growth" translate into the central dynamic of new learning leading to unique expertise. The feeling of satisfaction is also indicated as a dynamic of learning from clients and products.

The key to job enrichment is nurture of a client relationship rather than a functional or hierarchical relationship. Let me illustrate with a diagram of relationships in an airplane overhaul project carried out for the U.S. Air Force (*Figure C*). The avionics mechanic's external client is the test pilot, and although he reports to his supervisor, his supervisor serves him. The sheet metal mechanic and the line mechanic serve the avionics mechanic. And so on back into the system.

By backing into the system, you can identify who serves whom—not who reports to whom—which is critical in trying to enrich jobs. You identify the external client, then the core jobs, or internal client jobs, serving that client. You first enrich the core jobs with the ingredients shown in *Figure B* and then enrich the jobs that serve these internal clients.

During the 1970s, critics predicted that job enrichment would reduce the number of employees. Ironically, the restructuring and downsizing of U.S. companies during the 1980s have often serendipitously produced job enrichment. With fewer employees performing the same tasks, some job enrichment was inevitable. But the greater efficiency of enriched jobs ultimately leads to a competitive edge and more jobs.

Today, we seem to be losing ground to KITA. It's all the bottom line, as the expression goes. The work ethic and the quality

of worklife movement have succumbed to the pragmatics of worldwide competition and the escalation of management direction by the abstract fields of finance and marketing—as opposed to production and sales, where palpable knowledge of clients and products resides. These abstract fields are more conducive to movement than to motivation. I find the new entrants in the world of work on the whole a passionless lot intent on serving financial indexes rather than clients and products. Motivation encompasses passion; movement is sterile.

To return to "One More Time": I don't think I would write it much differently today, though I would include the knowledge gained from recent job enrichment experiments. The distinction between movement and motivation is still true, and motivation-hygiene theory is still a framework with which to evaluate actions. Job enrichment remains the key to designing work that motivates employees.

▶ Some workers are motivatable; some are not. How can the former be identified and developed? Here are the results of a six-year study at Texas Instruments.

Who Are Your Motivated Workers?

By M. Scott Myers

❰ What motivates employees to work effectively? *A challenging job which allows a feeling of achievement, responsibilty, growth, advancement, enjoyment of work itself, and earned recognition.*

❰ What dissatisfies workers? *Mostly factors which are peripheral to the job — work rules, lighting, coffee breaks, titles, seniority rights, wages, fringe benefits, and the like.*

❰ When do workers become dissatisfied? *When opportunities for meaningful achievement are eliminated and they become sensitized to their environment and begin to find fault.*

These and other interesting conclusions have been drawn from a six-year study of motivation research conducted at Texas Instruments Incorporated. This company's need for answers stemmed from its remarkable growth, for during the 1950's Texas Instruments grew from 1,700 to 17,000 employees, and from annual sales of $2 million to over $200 million. TI's take-off was sparked by a philosophy of management built on informal, shirt-sleeve relationships which fostered informal communication, company identification, and dedicated effort at all levels. Underlying this philosophy was the conviction that *company* goals could be best served by providing opportunities for employees to achieve their *personal* goals.

Highly motivated employees and managers found it easy during the growth years to overlook or take in stride existing and latent problems associated with supervisory ineptness and communication breakdowns. But when company growth decelerated in 1960, motivation ceased to be self-generating and became increasingly dependent on the skill of supervision.

Measure for Motivation

Starting in 1958, attempts were made to measure symptoms and causes of motivation and dissatisfaction among company workers. Results, unfortunately, were not easily translatable into remedial action. But in 1960, TI management's interest was aroused by some research done by Professor Frederick Herzberg, chairman of the Psychology Department of Western Reserve University. Herzberg's motivation analysis of engineers and accountants in the Pittsburgh area found that the levels of job satisfaction, motivation, and productivity of engineers and accountants were closely related to two sets of factors:

▼ *Dissatisfiers* are made up, essentially, of such matters as pay, supplemental benefits, company policy and administration, behavior of supervision, working conditions, and several other factors somewhat peripheral to the task. Though traditionally perceived by management as motivators of people, these factors were found to be more potent as dissatisfiers. High motivation does not result from their improvement, but dissatisfaction does result from their deterioration. Negative motivators can be dissatisfiers too, but not so frequently as the factors just given. For example, while *achievement* is a motivator, *failure to achieve* can, of course, be a dissatisfier.

▲ *Motivators*, for the most part, are the factors of achievement, recognition, responsibility, growth, advancement, and other matters associated with the self-actualization of the individual on the job. Job satisfaction and high production were associated with motivators, while disappointments and ineffectiveness were usually associated with dissatisfiers.

Since Herzberg's research presented a possible key to the motivation problem in TI, the company was eager to test whether his theory could be validly applied to its own workers.

Insights From Personnel

In 1961, research began at TI. From a list of employees chosen because of their representativeness, subjects were selected randomly, with the result that they were distributed almost equally over the three salaried job categories of scientist, engineer, and manufacturing supervisor and the two hourly paid classifications of technician and assembler. All 282 subjects were male (except 52 female hourly assemblers); and all were employed in the Dallas divisions.

A competent personnel administrator interviewed each of the subjects, beginning by explaining the general purpose of the project and the nature of the information required. Next, following Herzberg's interview pattern, the interviewer asked:

"Think of a time when you felt exceptionally good or exceptionally bad about your job, either your present job or any other job you have had. This can be either the 'long-range' or the 'short-range' kind of situation, as I have just described it. Tell me what happened."

After an employee's description of a sequence of events that he felt good about ("favorable") was completely explored, he was asked to tell of a different time when he felt the opposite ("unfavorable"); or, if he had first described an unfavorable sequence of events, he was asked

about a favorable sequence. Notes were taken during the interview, and questions interjected as necessary to obtain required details.

A total of 715 sequences were obtained from 282 interviewees — an average of 2.5 sequences per individual. Each of the 715 sequences was classified as "favorable" or "unfavorable" and as "long-range" (strong feelings lasting more than two months) or "short-range" (strong feelings lasting less than two months). As many as 54% of the sequences were favorable, while 59% were long-range. Exhibit I shows abbreviated examples of favorable and unfavorable sequences obtained for each of the five job categories we investigated. Employee responses were further broken down according to job category and sex of respondent. Following this, elements within the sequences were divided into:

• *First-level factors* — the actual events or circumstances leading to favorable or unfavorable feelings.

• *Second-level factors* — the explanations given by respondents as to *why* the event (the first-level factor) caused the favorable or unfavorable feelings.

First-Level Factors

Based on collective judgments of the interviewer and project head, 14 first-level factors were identified. Exhibit II lists these factors and the number of sequences grouped under each factor. It shows *achievement* to be the largest category, accounting for 33% of the sequences. *Achievement* is comprised of about twice as many favorable responses as unfavorable ones. Conversely, *company policy and administration* (the employee's perception of

EXHIBIT I. SAMPLE "FAVORABLE" AND "UNFAVORABLE" RESPONSES TO INTERVIEW QUESTIONS BY INCUMBENTS IN FIVE JOB CATEGORIES

SCIENTIST — FAVORABLE

About six months ago I was given an assignment to develop a new product. It meant more responsibility and an opportunity to learn new concepts. I had to study and learn. It was an entirely different job. I always enjoy learning something new. I had been in basic research where it's difficult to see the end results. Now I'm working much harder because I'm more interested. I'm better suited for this type of work.

SCIENTIST — UNFAVORABLE

In the fall of 1961 my group would find problems which needed work. We presented them to our supervisor, and he would say, "Don't bother me with details; we are in trouble in this area and need one person for guidance and I am this person." He assigns the problems. He said, "Do

EXHIBIT 1 *(continued)*

what I say whether you think it will work or not." I wouldn't come in Saturday. Made me want to go home and work on my yard. Negative attitude. Killed my initiative because no matter what I came up with my supervisor wouldn't accept it. At first we tried to convince him but finally gave up. Very few gains made in this environment.

ENGINEER — FAVORABLE

In 1959 I was working on a carefully outlined project. I was free to do as I saw fit. There was never a "no, you can't do this." I was doing a worthwhile job and was considered capable of handling the project. The task was almost impossible, but their attitude gave me confidence to tackle a difficult job. My accomplishments were recognized. It helped me gain confidence in how to approach a problem. It helped me to supervise a small number of people to accomplish a goal. I accomplished the project and gained something personally.

ENGINEER — UNFAVORABLE

In December 1961 I was disappointed in my increase. I was extremely well satisfied with the interview and rating. I was dejected and disillusioned, and I still think about it. I stopped working so much at night as a result of this increase. My supervisor couldn't say much. He tried to get me more money but couldn't get it approved.

MANUFACTURING SUPERVISOR — FAVORABLE

In September 1961 I was asked to take over a job which was thought to be impossible. We didn't think TI could ship what had been promised. I was told half would be acceptable, but we shipped the entire order! They had confidence in me to think I could do the job. I am happier when under pressure.

MANUFACTURING SUPERVISOR — UNFAVORABLE

In the fall of 1958 I disagreed with my supervisor. We were discussing how many of a unit to manufacture, and I told him I thought we shouldn't make too many. He said, "I didn't ask for your opinion . . . we'll do what I want." I was shocked as I didn't realize he had this kind of personality. It put me in bad with my supervisor and I resented it because he didn't consider my opinion important.

HOURLY MALE TECHNICIAN — FAVORABLE

In June 1961 I was given a bigger responsibility though no change in job grade. I have a better job, more interesting and one that fits in better with my education. I still feel good about it. I'm working harder because it was different from my routine. I am happier . . . feel better about my job.

HOURLY MALE TECHNICIAN — UNFAVORABLE

In 1962 I was working on a project and thought I had a real good solution. A professional in the group but not on my project tore down my project bit by bit in front of those I worked with. He made disparaging remarks. I was unhappy with the man and unhappy with myself. I thought I had solved it when I hadn't. My boss smoothed it over and made me feel better. I stayed away from the others for a week.

HOURLY FEMALE ASSEMBLER — FAVORABLE

About two weeks ago I wire-welded more transistors than anyone had ever done — 2,100 in nine hours. My foreman complimented me, and I still feel good. Meant self-satisfaction and peace of mind to know I'm doing a good job for them. Once you've done it, you want to do it every day, but you can't. It affected my feelings toward everyone. My old foreman came and talked to me. I didn't think I could ever wire-weld.

HOURLY FEMALE ASSEMBLER — UNFAVORABLE

For a while the foreman was partial to one of the girls on the line. She didn't work as hard as the other girls and made phone calls. It got to the point where we went to the man over her foreman and complained. We were all worried since we are afraid of reprisals. . . . The girls don't act the same toward each other now because they are afraid. It affects everyone's work. It has been going on for such a long time it's uncomfortable. It is being stopped now by the foreman's supervisor and that girl has been moved.

EXHIBIT II. FIRST-LEVEL FACTORS

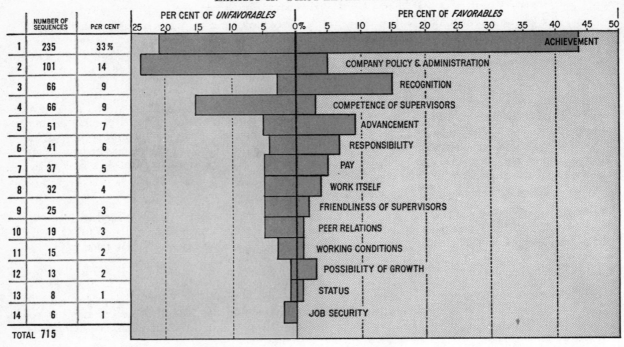

	NUMBER OF SEQUENCES	PER CENT	Factor
1	235	33%	ACHIEVEMENT
2	101	14	COMPANY POLICY & ADMINISTRATION
3	66	9	RECOGNITION
4	66	9	COMPETENCE OF SUPERVISORS
5	51	7	ADVANCEMENT
6	41	6	RESPONSIBILITY
7	37	5	PAY
8	32	4	WORK ITSELF
9	25	3	FRIENDLINESS OF SUPERVISORS
10	19	3	PEER RELATIONS
11	15	2	WORKING CONDITIONS
12	13	2	POSSIBILITY OF GROWTH
13	8	1	STATUS
14	6	1	JOB SECURITY
TOTAL	715		

company organization, goals, policies, procedures, practices, or rules) accounts for more than four times as many unfavorable as favorable responses. Since this exhibit includes data from *all five job categories*, it does not reflect differences among job categories. Consequently, a further category-by-category breakdown is necessary.

Personality Differences

But before the results of this analysis are presented, it is necessary that we point out that the potency of any of the job factors mentioned, as a motivator or dissatisfier, is not solely a function of the nature of the factor itself. It is also related to the personality of the individual.

For most individuals, the greatest satisfaction and the strongest motivation are derived from *achievement, responsibility, growth, advancement, work itself,* and *earned recognition.* People like this, whom Herzberg terms "motivation seekers," are motivated primarily by the nature of the task and have high tolerance for poor environmental factors.

"Maintenance seekers," on the other hand, are motivated primarily by the nature of their environment and tend to avoid motivation opportunities. They are chronically preoccupied and dissatisfied with maintenance factors surrounding the job, such as pay, supplemental benefits, supervision, working conditions, status, job security, company policy and administration, and fellow employees. Maintenance seekers realize little satisfaction from accomplishment and express cynicism regarding the positive virtues of work and life in general. By contrast, motivation seekers realize great satisfaction from accomplishment and have positive feelings toward work and life in general.

Maintenance seekers show little interest in kind and quality of work, may succeed on the job through sheer talent, but seldom profit professionally from experience. Motivation seekers enjoy work, strive for quality, tend to overachieve, and benefit professionally from experience.

Maintenance seekers are usually outer-directed and may be highly reactive or ultraconservative. Their values tend to blow with the wind and take on the coloring of the environment (such as parroting top management, or acting more like top management than top management itself). Motivation seekers are more often inner-directed, self-sufficient persons whose belief systems are deliberately chosen and developed, and are less subject to influence by the environment.

Although an individual's orientation as a motivation seeker or a maintenance seeker is fairly permanent, it can be influenced by the characteristics of his various roles. For example, maintenance seekers in an environment of achievement, responsibility, growth, and earned recognition tend to behave like and acquire the values of motivation seekers. On the other hand, the absence of motivators causes many motivation seekers to behave like maintenance seekers, and to become preoccupied with the maintenance factors in their environment.

All of the five occupational groups discussed below, except female assemblers, seem to be largely comprised of actual or potential motivation seekers. Scientists are the group most strongly oriented as motivation seekers, and female assemblers those most strongly oriented as maintenance seekers. Maintenance seeking among female assemblers probably stems from the tradition of circumscribed and dependent roles of women in industry as well as from their supervisors' failure to provide them with motivation opportunities.

Now let us examine each occupational group in detail.

Scientists

EXHIBIT III shows the distribution of first-level factors for scientists. The length of the **gray** bars on the upper side of the transparent horizontal plane indicates the percentage of favorable sequences or events classified under each factor. For example, 50% of the favor-

able sequences relate to achievement. The other 50% are distributed among the other six categories shown in **gray** on the upper side. Similarly, black bars on the lower side show the frequency distribution of "unfavorable" sequences. Factors whose combined "favorables" and "unfavorables" represented less than 5% of the sequences for a given job category have not been charted for that category.

Earlier the terms "motivators" and "dissatisfiers" were defined. In EXHIBIT III, those factors which extend predominantly above the plane are clearly "motivators," for these are not peripheral to the job itself. In fact, the motivators listed in this and the following charts relate to motivation needs which are *closely* associated with job performance. Bars extending predominantly below are "dissatisfiers," or maintenance factors, since their satisfaction serves to avoid dissatisfaction rather than to stimulate motivation, and since they are peripheral to the task.

The height of the bars in EXHIBIT III shows duration of feelings, based on the ratio of number of long-lasting to short-term feelings. The duration of feelings, in turn, reflects their relative importance to the individual. Note, in the case of scientists, that long-lasting good feelings are often associated with *work itself* and that

EXHIBIT III. FACTORS AFFECTING MOTIVATION OF SCIENTISTS

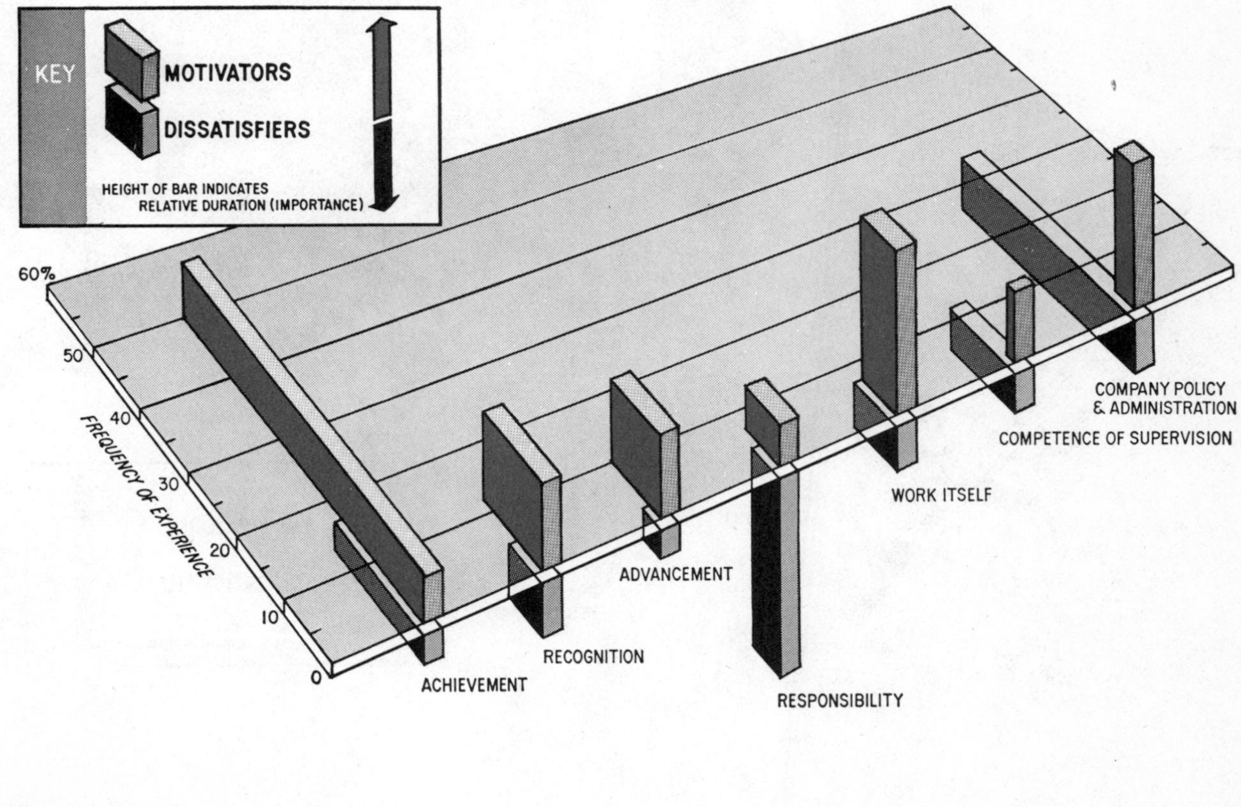

EXHIBIT IV-A. FACTORS AFFECTING MOTIVATION OF ENGINEERS

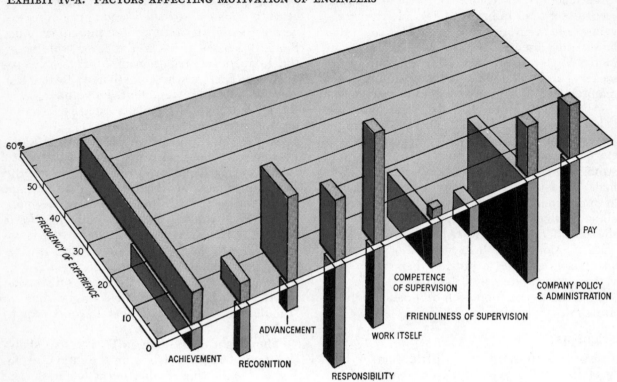

EXHIBIT IV-B. FACTORS AFFECTING MOTIVATION OF MANUFACTURING SUPERVISORS

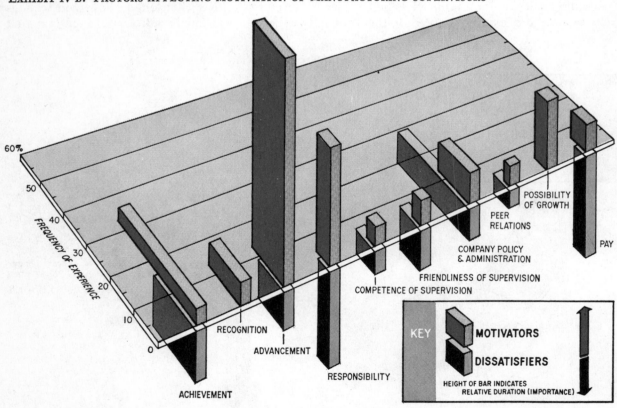

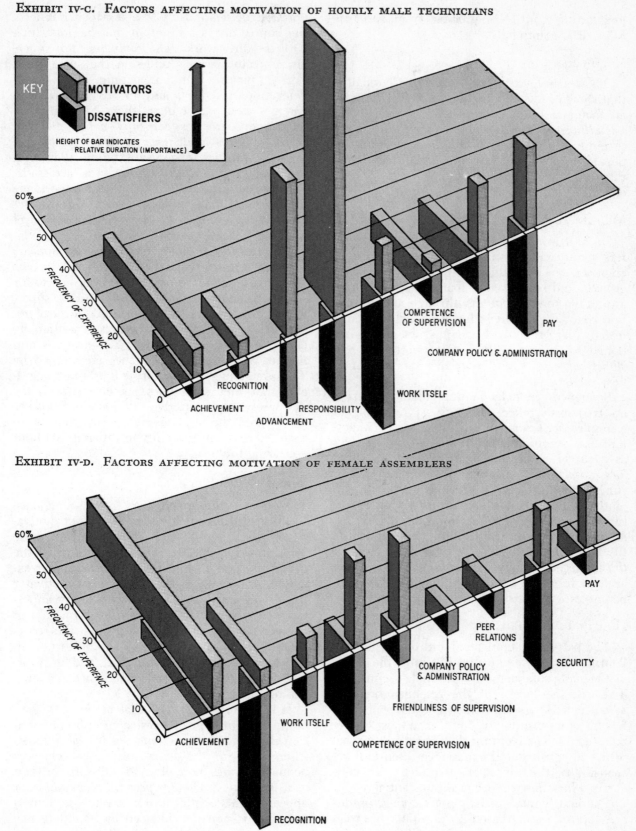

EXHIBIT IV-C. FACTORS AFFECTING MOTIVATION OF HOURLY MALE TECHNICIANS

EXHIBIT IV-D. FACTORS AFFECTING MOTIVATION OF FEMALE ASSEMBLERS

long-lasting bad feelings stem from *responsibility* disappointments.

Engineers

These employees reveal a pattern similar to that shown by scientists. EXHIBIT IV-A contains all factors found on the scientists' chart, plus *friendliness of supervision* and *pay.* This is not to imply that these two factors are not important to the scientists, but rather that they do not rate as high a priority in the scientists' hierarchy of needs.

Manufacturing Supervisors

In EXHIBIT IV-B we see a pattern which differs significantly from that of the scientists or engineers. The tallness of the *advancement, growth,* and *responsibility* bars reflects a higher aspiration toward success through administration than was apparent for scientists and engineers. Note that *work itself* is not even mentioned by manufacturing supervisors, but *possibility of growth* and *peer relations* appear as new factors.

Sequences cited by manufacturing supervisors frequently reflect climbing aspirations. For example, *achievement* is usually more important as a stepping stone to success, and *failure* as a threat to advancement. *Company policy and administration* as a maintenance factor functions as a block to advancement, and as a motivation factor it is seen as providing opportunity for achieving career objectives. *Peer relations* as a dissatisfier usually stems from the thwarting of career goals by associates. *Pay,* for the manager, usually signifies success or failure and, in terms of duration of feelings, is more potent as a dissatisfier than as a motivator.

Hourly Technicians

The pattern of motivators and dissatisfiers in EXHIBIT IV-C dramatically illustrates the needs of the semiprofessional hourly male technician. The extreme height of the responsibility and advancement bars shows the importance of these factors as motivators to him. Since most hourly paid technicians feel that they have little opportunity to advance and experience a sense of responsibility, the impact of these factors as motivators when they do occur is substantial.

The hourly man, usually not a college graduate, tends to see himself in a supportive role, doing the unpleasant and uninteresting tasks which professionals choose to avoid. The importance of *work itself* as a dissatisfier reflects the hourly man's contention that he gets stuck with the dirty work. The *competence of supervision* factor (which refers to the supervisor's skill in planning and organizing work, to his delegating practices, and to his impartiality) emerges as a potent dissatisfier. Similarly, the technician perceives *company policy and administration* as inadequate or unfair in providing opportunities for job satisfaction. *Pay* is an important factor, slightly more so as a dissatisfier than as a motivator. Its greater importance to the hourly male probably stems from the fact that he lives closer to the subsistence level than do salaried persons.

The technician chart (EXHIBIT IV-C) appears to reflect greater frustrations and hence greater challenge to supervision than do the charts for scientists, engineers, and manufacturing supervisors. Male technicians work at a level of responsibility where supervision is traditionally close. Being males with career aspirations and normal needs for independence (reinforced by TI's philosophy of equality), it is understandable that they sometimes perceive supervision as oppressively restrictive. Perhaps in no other group does the supervisor's success depend to such a degree on his ability to supervise without appearing to do so.

Female Assemblers

Motivators and dissatisfiers for the female assembler, as EXHIBIT IV-D shows, reflect motivational needs significantly different from those of other job categories. However, not all of the differences are evident from the chart. For example, *achievement,* the most potent motivator for all classifications, derives its primary importance for the female from the affirmation it wins from her supervisor. Note that the *recognition* bars show favorable recognition to be an important short-range motivator, and unfavorable recognition or the lack of recognition a long-lasting dissatisfier.

It is interesting to note that *work itself,* generally thought to be oppressively routine, is mentioned as often as a motivator as it is as a dissatisfier. *Pay* for the female assembler emerges about five times more often as a dissatisfier than as a motivator. Though *peer relations* does not appear in this exhibit as a motivator, its importance to women is evidenced by its emergence as a dissatisfier when friendly relationships break down. The height of the *competence of supervision* and the *friendliness of supervision* bars indicates the importance of fair, competent, and friendly supervision as satisfiers, and the impact of favoritism, incompetence, and unfriendliness as dissatisfiers. The height of the *security* bar as a dissatisfier probably reflects the lingering impact of layoffs which actually affected only a small number.

The total pattern of the hourly female chart indicates that, unlike the hourly male, she has not found advancement and increased responsibility potent motivators, and she tends to prefer close supervision. Her supervisor should be impartial, competent, decisive, and friendly. Despite women's cherished status of equality, most female assemblers seem to prefer to relate themselves to their supervisor in a dependent role. To these female assemblers, many of whom are single, widowed, or divorced, the supervisor is an important person (sometimes the only one) to whom she can turn for understanding, affirmation, and recognition.

Second-Level Factors

The factors just analyzed were those revealed by the respondent's description of the actual events leading to his favorable or unfavorable feelings. But this tells only part of the story. As noted, during the information-gathering interview, after the respondent had described a sequence, he was asked what the event *meant* to him, and *why* it made him feel good or bad.

The reasons he gave were recorded as second-level factors.

Each sequence usually resulted in two or more such second-level factors, one of which was often the same as a first-level factor. Thus, in 70% of those sequences where *achievement* was the first-level factor, it was also named as a second-level factor. Other second-level factors commonly resulting from achievement were *recognition, work itself, pride,* and *growth.* For instance:

The female assembler, mentioned in EXHIBIT I, who wire-welded 2,100 transistors illustrates the classification process. Her first-level factor was "achievement," and her second-level factors were "recognition," "achievement," and "pride." Achievement was first-level because, as she put it, "I didn't think I could ever wire-weld." But she did! She welded more than anyone had ever done before. However, the *importance* of the event for her stemmed from the second-level factors which she later identified as recognition, a feeling of achievement, and pride.

EXHIBIT V presents the distribution of the 1,255 responses of second-level factors resulting from the 715 sequences charted in EXHIBIT II; 9 of the 12 second-level factors also appeared as first-level factors. In EXHIBITS V through XII-B, combined data from all five job categories are given to shed light on the second-level factors which were identified for each of the 14 first-level factors. The pie charts indicate why a given factor is a motivator or dissatisfier (by

EXHIBIT V. SECOND-LEVEL FACTORS

	NUMBER OF SEQUENCES	PER CENT		
1	337	27%		ACHIEVEMENT
2	181	14		RECOGNITION
3	147	12		WORK ITSELF
4	141	11		FAIRNESS
5	91	7		GROUP FEELING
6	81	6		RESPONSIBILITY
7	80	6		POSSIBILITY OF GROWTH
8	53	4		PAY
9	53	4		JOB SECURITY
10	37	3		PRIDE
11	34	3		STATUS
12	20	2		ADVANCEMENT
	TOTAL 1,255			

PER CENT OF *UNFAVORABLES*: 25 20 15 10 5 0% — PER CENT OF *FAVORABLES*: 0% 5 10 15 20 25 30 35 40

showing the distribution of second-level factors for the first-level experience). The page-wide horizontal charts portray the first-level factors which contributed to a particular second-level feeling.

Achievement & Failure

EXHIBIT VI-A reveals that *achievement* is its own best reward; this is evidenced by the fact successful achievement stem from a successful achievement in 63% of the cases. The potency of other, seemingly unrelated experiences in causing feelings of achievement in workers is largely a function of individual needs. For example, the realization of a specific personal goal may be felt to be an achievement only by the person affected.

Unlike feelings of achievement, which stem

EXHIBIT VI-A. WHY ACHIEVEMENT IS A MOTIVATOR

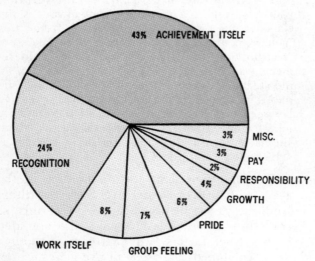

EXHIBIT VI-B. WHY FAILURE IS A DISSATISFIER

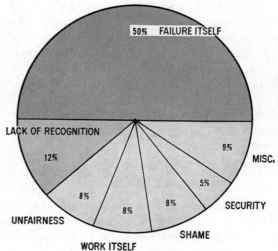

that "achievement itself" constitutes 43% of the reasons given as to why an achievement was gratifying.

EXHIBIT VI-B indicates that *failure* (with 50%) is a dissatisfier for essentially the same reasons that achievement is a motivator. Only *unfairness* and *security* emerge as new factors.

EXHIBIT VII-A, which portrays the first-level factors which caused the second-level feelings of achievement, bears out the adage that "nothing succeeds like success," since feelings of

from an act of the doer in about two-thirds of the first-level achievement sequences, feelings of failure usually arise from external forces. As EXHIBIT VII-B shows, in only 32% of the cases do feelings of failure originate from workers' acknowledged personal failures on the job.

Recognition

Both motivation and maintenance needs are served by *recognition*. Earned recognition is a manifestation of justice, an act of approv-

EXHIBIT VII-A. FACTORS CONTRIBUTING TO FEELINGS OF ACHIEVEMENT

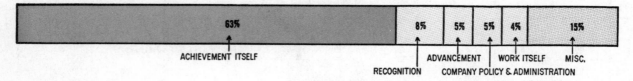

EXHIBIT VII-B. FACTORS CONTRIBUTING TO FEELINGS OF FAILURE

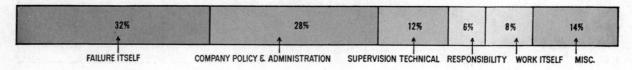

EXHIBIT VIII-A. WHY RECOGNITION IS A MOTIVATOR

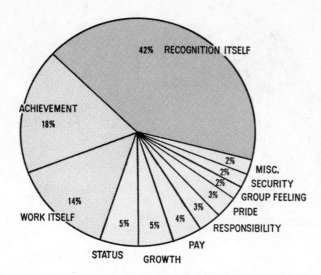

EXHIBIT VIII-B. WHY RECOGNITION IS A DISSATIS-FIER

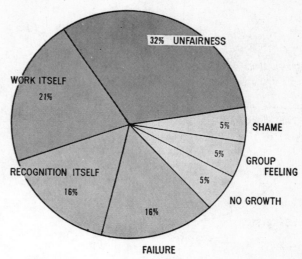

al which confirms successful achievement and individual worth. Pay increases and bonuses stemming from merit are tangible acts of recognition. And these are usually potent as motivators for motivation seekers and as dissatisfiers for maintenance seekers.

Unearned recognition, in the form of friendliness, reassurance, small talk, and personal interest, serves to satisfy security, status, and social needs. This type of recognition is not a substitute for earned recognition, but it is essential as a maintenance factor, particularly in the absence of opportunity to earn recognition through job performance.

But recognition as a sustaining force has little lasting value, as evidenced by the shortness of the *security* bars in EXHIBITS III through IV-D. Its potency as a motivator, in view of its short duration, indicates a need for frequent reinforcement. On the other hand, recognition for scientists (EXHIBIT III) frequently arises from professional activities and tends to be somewhat longer lasting. The need for meaningful interim recognition for scientists on long-range projects is obvious, and professional activities often serve this need.

EXHIBIT VIII-A shows recognition to be a prime catalyst for other motivational experiences, with recognition itself the most commonly mentioned second-level factor. Perhaps recognition as an end product derives much of its value from the fact that for many workers who personally see only a miniscule portion of the total task, recognition is the only criterion of achievement and progress available to them.

EXHIBIT VIII-B shows the consequences of unfavorable recognition or the failure to receive expected recognition. Recognition disappointments result in dissatisfactions associated with unfairness, work itself, recognition itself, failure, stymied growth, hostility toward the work group, and shame. The double-edged potential of recognition reflected in these two charts offers no support to the philosophy expressed in the cliché, "If they don't hear from me, they know they're doing O.K."

Pay Itself

The role of pay as an incentive is controversial. EXHIBITS III through IV-D show pay itself not to be particularly influential as either a motivator or dissatisfier. EXHIBITS IX-A and IX-B indicate that pay derives its importance primarily from the factors it represents. In EXHIBIT IX-A *pay itself* accounts for only 11% of the reasons for satisfaction and is only one-fourth as important as the recognition it represents. EXHIBIT IX-B indicates that a disappointment in pay has more impact as an act of unfairness than it has as a loss of pay itself. From comparison of the relative percentages of pay itself on the two charts it appears that pay itself is less potent as a motivator than as a dissatisfier.

Work Itself

Attitudes toward *work itself* are related less to the nature of the task than they are to other factors in the work situation. EXHIBIT X-A indicates that a good feeling toward work itself stems from the nature of the task in only 8% of

EXHIBIT IX-A. WHY PAY IS A MOTIVATOR

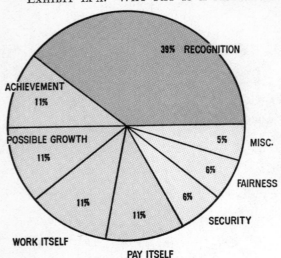

EXHIBIT IX-B. WHY PAY IS A DISSATISFIER

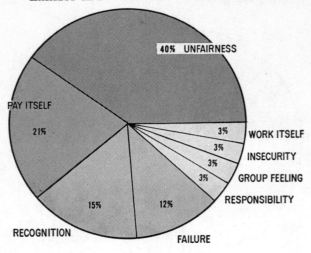

EXHIBIT X-A. FACTORS CONTRIBUTING TO SATISFACTION WITH WORK ITSELF

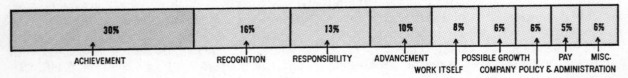

EXHIBIT X-B. FACTORS CONTRIBUTING TO DISSATISFACTION WITH WORK ITSELF

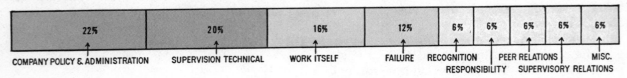

the cases. However, work itself plus all other motivators on the chart accounts for 80% of the good feelings associated with work itself. By contrast, EXHIBIT X-B indicates that disenchantment with work itself results more often from maintenance factors.

Fairness

Positive *fairness* is a negligible second-level factor. On the other hand, *unfairness* is designated by female assemblers more often than any other second-level factor as the reason for

unhappiness on the job. Male respondents designate unfairness second only to failure as the explanation of feelings of unhappiness.

EXHIBIT XI reveals that feelings of unfairness are most commonly associated with three times as many maintenance factors as are motivation factors.

Supervision

Although supervisory competence and supervisory relations are discussed as two discrete first-level factors, they are inextricably related

EXHIBIT XI. FACTORS CONTRIBUTING TO FEELINGS OF UNFAIRNESS

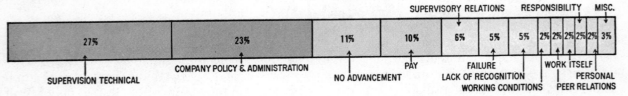

to all other first- and second-level factors. Supervisory competence, for example, manifested as delegation, planning and organizing work, and impartiality, has a bearing on the potency of motivators and dissatisfiers in the job environment as evidenced by EXHIBITS XII-A and XII-B.

EXHIBIT XII-A. WHY GOOD SUPERVISION IS A MOTIVATOR

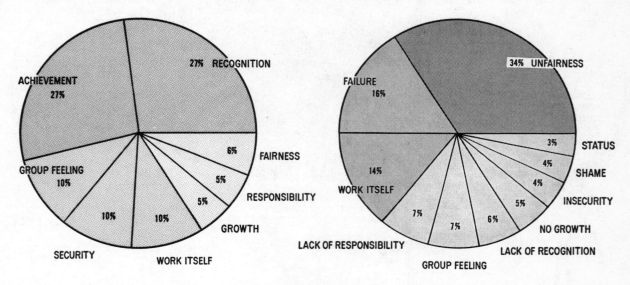

EXHIBIT XII-A. WHY GOOD SUPERVISION IS A MOTIVATOR

EXHIBIT XII-B. WHY POOR SUPERVISION IS A DISSATISFIER

The first of these exhibits indicates that good feelings about supervision are translated into motivators in three-fourths of the cases, most potent of which are recognition and achievement. Poor supervision as a first-level factor, as EXHIBIT XII-B shows, results in unhappiness associated with dissatisfiers in more than half the cases.

Wellsprings of Motivation

This study clearly points out that the factors in the work situation which motivate employees are different from the factors that dissatisfy employees. Motivation stems from the challenge of the job through such factors as achievement, responsibility, growth, advancement, work itself, and earned recognition. Dissatisfactions more often spring from factors peripheral to the task.

Effective job performance depends on the fulfillment of both motivation and maintenance needs. Motivation needs, as EXHIBIT XIII illustrates, include responsibility, achievement, recognition, and growth, and are satisfied through the media grouped in the inner circle of the exhibit. Motivation factors focus on the individual

and his achievement of company and personal goals.

Maintenance needs are satisfied through media listed in the outer circle under the headings of physical, social, status, orientation, security, and economic. Peripheral-to-the-task and usually group-administered maintenance factors have little motivational value, but their fulfillment is essential to the avoidance of dissatisfaction. An environment rich in opportunities for satisfying motivation needs leads to motivation-seeking habits, and a job situation sparse in motivation opportunities encourages preoccupation with maintenance factors.

In other words, in a situation of satisfied motivation needs, maintenance factors have relatively little influence either as satisfiers or dissatisfiers. However, the removal of opportunity for meaningful achievement sensitizes the individual to his environment, and his perception of maintenance factors becomes colored by a readiness to find fault.

Thus motivation, or the achievement of personal goals, is not facilitated by management actions which overrate maintenance needs, but rather by actions which provide conditions of motivation.

The spiraling cost of fringe benefits in business and industry cries out that management is continually making misguided and futile attempts to motivate through maintenance factors. Competition among companies to outdo each other in the realm of maintenance factors,

EXHIBIT XIII. EMPLOYEE NEEDS — MAINTENANCE AND MOTIVATIONAL

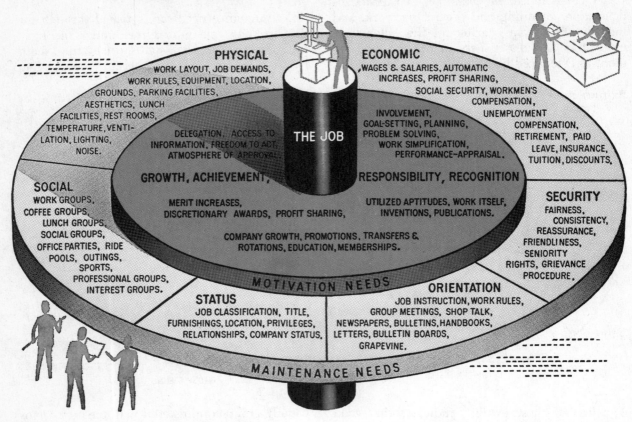

PHYSICAL
WORK LAYOUT, JOB DEMANDS, WORK RULES, EQUIPMENT, LOCATION, GROUNDS, PARKING FACILITIES, AESTHETICS, LUNCH FACILITIES, REST ROOMS, TEMPERATURE, VENTILATION, LIGHTING, NOISE.

ECONOMIC
WAGES & SALARIES, AUTOMATIC INCREASES, PROFIT SHARING, SOCIAL SECURITY, WORKMEN'S COMPENSATION, UNEMPLOYMENT COMPENSATION, RETIREMENT, PAID LEAVE, INSURANCE, TUITION, DISCOUNTS.

THE JOB

DELEGATION, ACCESS TO INFORMATION, FREEDOM TO ACT, ATMOSPHERE OF APPROVAL.

INVOLVEMENT, GOAL-SETTING, PLANNING, PROBLEM SOLVING, WORK SIMPLIFICATION, PERFORMANCE–APPRAISAL.

GROWTH, ACHIEVEMENT,
MERIT INCREASES, DISCRETIONARY AWARDS, PROFIT SHARING,

RESPONSIBILITY, RECOGNITION
UTILIZED APTITUDES, WORK ITSELF, INVENTIONS, PUBLICATIONS.

COMPANY GROWTH, PROMOTIONS, TRANSFERS & ROTATIONS, EDUCATION, MEMBERSHIPS.

SOCIAL
WORK GROUPS, COFFEE GROUPS, LUNCH GROUPS, SOCIAL GROUPS, OFFICE PARTIES, RIDE POOLS, OUTINGS, SPORTS, PROFESSIONAL GROUPS, INTEREST GROUPS.

SECURITY
FAIRNESS, CONSISTENCY, REASSURANCE, FRIENDLINESS, SENIORITY RIGHTS, GRIEVANCE PROCEDURE.

MOTIVATION NEEDS

STATUS
JOB CLASSIFICATION, TITLE, FURNISHINGS, LOCATION, PRIVILEGES, RELATIONSHIPS, COMPANY STATUS.

ORIENTATION
JOB INSTRUCTION, WORK RULES, GROUP MEETINGS, SHOP TALK, NEWSPAPERS, BULLETINS, HANDBOOKS, LETTERS, BULLETIN BOARDS, GRAPEVINE.

MAINTENANCE NEEDS

justifiable as it may seem as a competitive measure, fails to increase productivity and probably contributes to the pricing of American products and services out of the world market.

Paradoxically, satisfying motivation needs is not only the more realistic approach for satisfying personal goals and sustaining the organization, but it is also less expensive. The requirements for satisfying motivation needs are competent supervision or perpetual organizational growth. And growth without competent supervision, except in the case of temporary advantage from technological breakthrough or monopoly, is an unrealistic expectation.

The Supervisor's Role

Simply stated, the supervisor's role is twofold. He must:

1. Provide conditions of motivation.
2. Satisfy maintenance needs.

Conditions of motivation are task-centered; they depend on supervisors' skill in planning and organizing work. Ideally, the planning and organization of work begin at the top, to pro-

vide members at each succeeding organizational level with responsibilities, which in turn can be subdivided into meaningful chunks that challenge capabilities and satisfy aspirations. Matching jobs with people requires a knowledge and control of the task, as well as an understanding of individual aptitudes and aspirations.

Satisfaction of the motivation needs in EXHIBIT XIII is typically achieved through the mechanisms and media listed in the lower portion of the inner band. In terms of day-to-day behavior patterns, the role of the competent supervisor includes providing each individual with the requisite job information, maintaining high performance expectations, encouraging goal-setting and the exercise of independent judgment, providing recognition and rewards commensurate with achievements, and maintaining an atmosphere of approval in which failure is a basis for growth rather than recrimination.

The maintenance needs listed in EXHIBIT XIII as economic, security, orientation, status, social, and physical, have many conditions and media for satisfying these needs listed beneath them.

The supervisor's support in satisfying these needs is essential, particularly so for security and orientation needs. Feelings of security are largely influenced by the supervisor and determine whether the individual will assert himself in a constructive motivation-seeking manner, or will fall back on maintenance-seeking behavior. The satisfaction of orientation needs requires supervisors steeped in company lore, policies, procedures, and practices. The ability and willingness of supervisors to dispense information when requested meets a need seldom satisfied by handbooks and other written communications. Further, this information-dispensing role of the supervisor, served with friendly small talk, keeps communication channels open.

A Practical Application

Rapidly changing industry no longer affords time for the young supervisor to develop competence through an extended trial-and-error apprenticeship. Furthermore, in view of today's increasing technological orientation to business, he is often selected because of his professional competence with hardware. This only increases his need for a simple and practical theory of management that will accelerate his acquisition of managerial know-how.

The concept of maintenance and motivation needs developed here is not strange or abstract but is clearly part of the experience and repertoire of most supervisors, including the straw-boss supervisor of unskilled workers. Moreover, it is easily translatable to supervisory action at all levels of responsibility. It is a framework on which supervisors can evaluate and put into perspective the constant barrage of "helpful hints" to which they are subjected, and hence serves to increase their feelings of competence, self-confidence, and autonomy.

Naturally, to become fully effective, motivation-maintenance theory must find expression in the day-to-day behavior and decisions of supervisors. For those supervisors whose personal adjustment and intuitive judgment endow them with natural aptitude for effective supervision, motivation-maintenance theory offers additional insights and guidance for reinforcing and further developing leadership skills. For them, motivation-maintenance theory finds almost immediate expression. For others, adopting and practicing this approach require an evolutionary process whereby (1) awareness, (2) understanding, (3) conviction, and (4) habit are developed over a period of perhaps five years.

Several mechanisms have been developed in TI to introduce this understanding to supervisors, to reinforce its application, and to audit its effectiveness.

TI's corporate ten-year plan for personnel administration (which is updated annually to support the ten-year operating goals of the corporation) was restructured in 1963 to fit motivation-maintenance theory concepts. Functions performed by personnel were analyzed in terms of their potential for serving maintenance or motivation needs. Next, both the theory and the research on which it was based were thoroughly explained to managers and supervisors at all levels through the medium of large group meetings. Here also these men were informed of the company's plan to implement the theory, and their cooperation was elicited.

Since satisfying employee maintenance needs requires that a company pay attention to the environmental factors shown on the outer circle of EXHIBIT XIII, TI closely examined how effectively newspapers, handbooks, group meetings, wages and salaries, safety and health services, social and recreational programs, and the like were meeting workers' needs.

In order to facilitate the meeting of motivation needs, a training program for supervisors, entitled Seminar in Motivation, was presented to all levels of supervision. Meeting in groups of from six to ten men, supervisors assimilated the theory and gained skills in its application to problems related to their own supervisory responsibility in a series of six two-hour sessions. The intense personal involvement of supervisors in the meetings and initial feedback from their subordinates indicate that these working sessions will meet long-felt needs and result in more effective supervision.

Attitude Survey

Quality of supervision is reflected in job performance, attendance, morale, and ultimately in profits. However, these factors seldom lend themselves to timely or accurate measurement. Since employee attitudes are measurable predictors of behavior, a formalized attitude measurement program structured around the motivation-maintenance frame of reference has been instituted in TI. By this means, total company effectiveness in each of the six maintenance- and the four motivation-need areas can be appraised. A deficiency in one of these need areas, such as security or orientation, signals a need for reinforcing efforts in that area. Administered annually to 10% samples of each of the sixty-odd departments, the attitude survey yields trend data as well as interdepartmental comparisons, and is both a meaningful barometer of supervisory effectiveness and a key to corrective action.

Application and reinforcement of motivation-maintenance theory are also achieved through many other specific media such as performance appraisal, educational assistance, supervisors' newsletters, planning conferences, work simplification, wage and salary administration, statements of policy and procedure, and the maintenance of a system of democratic and informal relationships.

In the final analysis, the workability of a theory of management depends on its integration into the total management process. Further, motivation-maintenance theory, like any theory of management, is at the mercy of its practitioners and will remain intact and find effective utilization only to the extent that it serves as a mechanism for harnessing constructive motives.

It can be useful as a practical framework for codifying intuitive effectiveness and for guiding the inexperienced, but it will not correct a management failure which, for example, permits the appointment of immature or unscrupulous supervisors. The management philosophy which sparked the growth of TI created a fertile environment for introducing motivation–maintenance theory as a mechanism for achieving company goals by providing opportunities for employees to achieve personal goals.

EXECUTIVES AND ORGANIZATIONS

Real Work

by Abraham Zaleznik

Too many executives labor under a misapprehension about the nature of executive work because they do not clearly understand that guiding an organization is not synonymous with leadership. We may recognize leadership when we see it, but its true nature is hidden in common misconceptions about organizations, human nature, and the substance of executive work. Worse, these misconceptions keep many able people from developing as leaders. And they subordinate real work–the work of thinking about and acting on products, markets, and customers–to psychopolitics.

To understand how we got into this mess, let's start not in the executive suite but in New Guinea–in the Trobriand Islands to be precise, where for generations the natives engaged in a ritual called Kula, the exchange of beads while bartering for food and other valuables.

The natives' barter, as Fritz Roethlisberger long ago pointed out in his widely read classic *Management and Morale*, was the group's purposeful, logical work, while the exchange of beads was its social, nonlogical activity. But the natives themselves made no distinction between the two and gave equal weight to both activities. They worked hard, building canoes and harvesting crops to have the goods to barter. At the same time, they saved beads and exchanged them with their partners according to strict, yet implicit, rules of social conduct.

The beads were not a medium of exchange. Nor did the natives hoard them or use them as ornaments to display their rank within

In most companies, process and politics get more attention than leadership.

Abraham Zaleznik is the Konosuke Matsushita Professor of Leadership at the Harvard Business School, a psychoanalyst, and the author of five previous HBR articles, including "Managers and Leaders: Are They Different?" (May-June 1977). His book, The Managerial Mystique: Restoring Leadership in Business, *will be published by Harper & Row in May 1989.*

the group. The rules of the Kula established well-understood expectations about social standing. The mode of exchange insured that the beads acquired in one transaction would be held and admired for a short time only, then passed along in the course of more giving and receiving. Thus, from a purely functional perspective, exchanging beads merely facilitated the real work of the society, which was the production and barter of goods. In fact, the beads were the way the natives expressed their allegiance to the tribe and their willingness to go along with its rules and expectations.

Like the Trobrianders, we too have tribal rituals, ways in which we symbolically express our membership in organizations and our willingness to meet the expectations of others. And, like them, we are capable of doing real work, work that is equivalent to making canoes and raising crops. But unlike our primitive cousins, we too often subordinate the challenges of real work to the demands of psychopolitics – to balancing the rational and irrational expectations that others place on us. Social relations and office politics get more attention than customers and clients. Managers are measured by how well they get people to go along with the company's expectations, not by how well the company performs. Executives are preoccupied with coordination and control.

The experts got it wrong – getting people to cooperate is not the executive's real work.

The subordination of real work to psychopolitics is the understandable – but unintended – outgrowth of two separate phenomena. One is the evolution of large complex organizations in which executives must play many roles and cooperation is truly hard to foster. The other is the great success the human relations school of management has had in uncovering the social aspects of organizations and teaching them to executives.

During the 1930s, researchers, academics, and consultants began to look at business organizations not simply as technical or economic systems but as social systems – systems built on the expectations that individuals have about their place in the organization, their rights and obligations, and their mutual dependencies. Social systems are not the result of conscious planning (as, for example, a decentralized organization structure would be), but rather exist as a result of human proclivities, of all the unwritten contracts that grow up between a company and its employees. Hence every organization has nonlogical underpinnings as well as logical ones – an informal pecking order, for instance, as well as the formal organization chart.

To sharpen this conception of organizations, human relations researchers focused next on the conditions of cooperation, the things managers could do to enhance workplace harmony. Under their tutelage, managers learned to diagnose breakdowns in cooperation by looking for ways in which the formal, logical system was violating important requirements of the informal social organization. A change in the organization's formal structure might trigger a rebellion, for example, not because subordinates objected to the actual content or purpose of the change but because it upset the informal hierarchy of the workplace. And this analysis would hold, the experts taught, whether the subordinates were managers and professionals in corporate offices or workers on the factory floor.

Managers' sensitivity to social relations in the workplace was further heightened by the growing difficulty of achieving cooperation in ever larger corporations. Much of the problem was simply a function of size. But investigators of modern managerial work and its discontents paid less attention to that than to technology and hierarchy, which, they argued, isolate people in their work. Isolation, in turn, creates problems of cooperation because it keeps people from developing normal social relations. Workers become more alienated from managers; managers become more alienated from their peers. For many, work becomes stressful; for some, downright unbearable. Pathological outcomes multiply: absenteeism, turnover, and, perhaps even worse, apathy, indifference, and the reluctance to exert any more energy or effort than the bare minimum needed to get by.

From diagnoses such as these, the human relations school gradually shaped a new definition of managerial work: developing and maintaining a system of cooperation. This definition included all those activities concerned with fostering communication, placing people in a coherent organization structure, and maintaining an informal executive organization. It also covered motivating people to perform services for the organization and formulating the organization's purpose and objectives.

In *The Functions of the Executive*, published in 1938, Chester I. Barnard called this array of activities "executive work." Conversely, what I call "real work"—specialized activities such as marketing, research, production—fell into the category of non-executive work because it did not *directly* address those elements in the workplace that affect cooperation. From the perspective of Barnard and his followers, therefore, technical and substantive activity came to look more and more like mere mechanics.

In my view, this conception of executive work led to an unhealthy preoccupation with process at the expense of productivity. Of course process and procedures are important: they establish the conditions for organizational cooperation and determine whether or not that cooperation will actually be achieved. In addition, they also influence deeply how effective executives will be in coordinating and controlling the work of others in the organization. But process and procedures are not the substance of the business, and they should not get as much—or more—attention than the work of the business itself.

Nevertheless, the human relations school was right on the basic point: organizations are indeed social systems, arenas for inducing cooperative behavior. And as such, they are quintessentially human and fraught with all the frailties and imperfections associated with the human condition. So much so, in fact, that one especially wise chief executive officer once commented, "Anyone in charge of an organization with more than two people is running a clinic."

The truth of this wry comment comes from the fact that while people want to cooperate, they also want to control their own destiny. And it is this universal desire to control our own destiny that creates conflicts of interest within organizations. At the same time, of course, it also stirs up conflict on a smaller, more personal scale.

Because people come together to satisfy a wide array of psychological needs, social relations in general are awash with conflict. In the course of their interactions, people must deal with differences as well as similarities, with aversions as well as affinities. Indeed, in

Freud had it right— people are like porcupines.

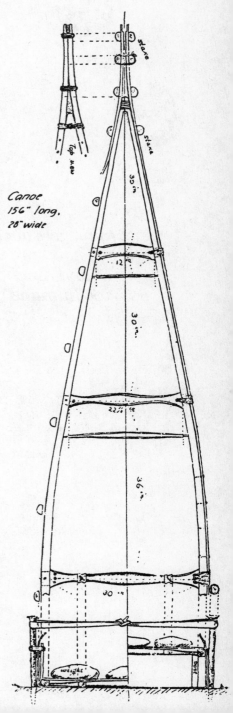

Canoe 156" long, 28" wide

Most managers are polite, considerate— and much too humane.

social relations, Sigmund Freud's parallel of humans and porcupines is apt: like porcupines, people will prick and injure one another if they get too close; they will feel cold if they get too far apart.

This complexity in human nature—especially our conflicting tendencies to cooperate and to go it alone—leads managers to spend their time smoothing over conflict, greasing the wheels of human interaction, and unconsciously avoiding aggression, especially aggression that centers on them and their role. The result is a seemingly permanent cleavage between substance and process in organizations, as managers struggle to maintain both the peace and their balance of power. Moreover, this cleavage imposes a Gresham-like law on organizations, for just as bad money drives out good, so psychopolitics drives out real work. People can focus their attention on only so many things. The more it lands on politics, the less energy—emotional and intellectual—is available to attend to the problems that fall under the heading of real work.

To complicate matters further, another basic fact about the human condition also enters into all considerations about work, real and nonreal alike. That is the sensitive relationship between anxiety and self-esteem. Anxiety is that awful feeling in the pit of your stomach when uncertainty reigns and fear of the future abounds. People don't tolerate anxiety well. Its appearance is a signal to do something to protect our integrity, to preserve our identity.

The need to act in the face of anxiety is as prevalent in a modern organization as in a primitive tribe, although both the causes of anxiety and the way people experience it differ. In a tribal ritual such as the Kula, primitive people exchange gifts as a way of dealing with anxiety about the future. The fear is a basic one: What if barter and exchange give way to aggression and hostility? What if one group goes after another and seeks to conquer? To relieve this anxiety, the groups exchange beads and thereby signify their intention to respect the peaceful alliance. More energy can go into real work, less into defense from the threat of danger.

For individuals in preliterate societies, danger is always external: a bad storm during a fishing expedition or warfare among neighbors is punishment from the gods for some transgression or failure in obeisance. People in modern societies are more or less conscious of the distinction between internal and external danger. Indeed, the more educated people are, the less they tend to project their ills onto the outside world. They are more inclined to blame themselves for their anxiety, experience guilt and shame in reaction to perceived shortcomings, and often require considerable support to rebuild diminished self-esteem. In this cycle of self-blame, they seek support from authority, and whether they get it or not, they often suffer a reduced capacity for real work.

Recognizing another's struggles with anxiety—and dealing with the morale problems that inevitably ensue—puts a call on the manager's capacity for empathy. It also challenges his or her social skills, particularly the ability to reduce tensions in groups. The current idealization of management reflects these social and human demands. Few managers today behave as autocrats. As a group, they are exceedingly polite, considerate of others, egalitarian in their behavior, and sincerely interested in making other people comfortable with the differences in power that exist in every organization. But this humane style of management poses at least two kinds of problems in the interaction between real work and the balancing acts of psychopolitics.

The first problem appears in the doubts that frequently arise about the nature of managerial competence. While no hard data exist, observation tells me that too many managers put interpersonal matters, power relations, and pouring oil on troubled waters ahead of real work. While generally active in their jobs, they avoid aggression (to use the Freudian term) like the plague. They don't go on the offensive themselves, even if that means unconsciously suppressing constructive criticism. Nor do they encourage conflict among subordinates or peers.

On the surface, this tendency appears to be a useful way to assure cooperation. But as with all things human, it has unintended consequences for the managers themselves and for their organizations. Followers tend to take their cues from authority figures. So if the leader's style is low-key, followers too will suppress aggression. Before long, group norms will appear to foster the appearances of getting along and to discourage individuality. Process takes precedence over substance. Attention turns inward to the organization's politics rather than outward to the real work of making and marketing goods and services.

For individuals, the costs are equally high because aggressive energy channeled into real work is the one sure route to a sense of mastery, to the pleasure that comes from using one's talents to accomplish things. In fact, without the application of aggression, little real work would ever get done. Of course, aggression can be misdirected. It can be turned inward and experienced as depression, with accompanying feelings of guilt and diminished self-worth. Or it can be turned on people with whom one should ostensibly be allied. But aggression is too valuable an emotion— and too basic a human drive—to suppress merely because it can be misdirected.

The second problem that arises from a disproportionate emphasis on social relations also relates to subordinates' reactions. In the 1930s, the Austrian-born psychiatrist J.L. Moreno uncovered the simple, yet profound fact that followers differentiate between task leaders and social leaders. Given a choice, they would prefer to be friends with people who characteristically ease the tensions that arise in group relations. But they would not choose to work with these specialists in tension reduction. Conversely, they would choose to work with people they identify as proficient; but they would not choose to have them for friends.

Experiments in social psychology and observations of so-called natural groups have since corroborated Moreno's discovery. In primitive cultures that transfer authority patrilineally, for example, the young male will respect but keep his distance from his father, who is responsible for providing food and shelter. For an easier relationship with an adult male, he will choose his mother's brother, following the kinship that provides nurture, affection, and comfort.

This suggests that the ideal solution—one that promotes real work and provides for the expressive and supportive components of group relations—would be to foster two kinds of leadership in two

Without aggression, little real work would ever get done.

The self-confidence born of competence builds cohesion and morale.

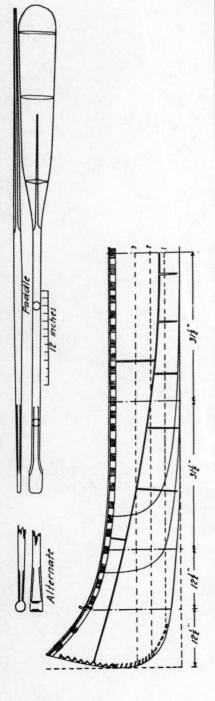

different individuals: a task leader and a social leader. Not surprisingly, such splits often occur spontaneously. The chairman acts as the organization's social leader, for example, while the president serves as the task leader who focuses attention on real work. But cultivating dual leadership leads to questionable results, because it reflects—and amplifies—the emphasis that is placed on seeking and maintaining cooperation even at the expense of superior performance in real work. Nothing will kill a middle manager's chances for promotion faster, for example, than a reputation for being "aggressive" (or worse, "abrasive"). But doesn't "aggressive" often really mean energetic, persistent, and goal oriented?

The end point of this analysis is not to encourage conflict and disharmony. It does suggest the need to look carefully at why real work generates respect and support from colleagues and subordinates and also overcomes the anxiety people often experience in hard-driving situations. I believe that executives who are superior in performing real work overcome this anxiety, not because someone else drains off any tension or hostility, but because there is something inherently humanizing about the use of talent to get things done.

Humankind does not live by bread alone but also by catchphrases. Thus the definition of management as "getting things done through other people" is often refined by the popular old saw that "the best salesman doesn't make the best sales manager." Now, it's certainly true that managing is more than applying technical proficiency. But it also makes simple good sense to suppose that substantive talent is an invaluable asset—perhaps even the crucial building block—in developing managers who will become leaders.

Without attributing too much to Japan's current industrial ascendancy, it is worth asking why leading Japanese companies recruit and train their factory supervisors (and I mean front-line supervisors) from the ranks of graduate engineers. The answer, I believe, is self-confidence—the self-confidence of managers who have demonstrated mastery in the substance of their work. This self-confidence induces confidence in others. And by itself, confidence builds cohesion and morale. A feeling of optimism accompanies the knowledge, gained from firsthand experience, that the person in charge knows what he or she is doing. Indeed, the demise of the conglomerates illustrates the point in reverse: it never took more than a step or two up the authority ladder before a division head encountered a boss who had little idea—and even less concern—for the substance of the division's work.

Making substance the leading edge of executive work means applying one or more talents, or business imaginations. Imaginations differ in business. The marketing imagination relies on empathy with the customer and on the capacity to visualize what products, services, and applications will make life better for the customer. The manufacturing imagination is driven by the proposition that there is a better way to apply energies in the man-machine relationship and searches constantly for the better way. The financial imagination is impelled by the idea that market disjunctions create opportunities and seeks to take advantage of them.

An underlying aggressiveness drives all business imaginations. Typically, the executive takes a position: "We will cut prices, promote to increase market share, build a direct distribution network, and end our reliance on independent distributors." Or "We're going to get out of this business because it's a commodity." Or "We're in a business that depends on being cost-effective. So we're going to spend money on research to improve our manufacturing techniques, increase productivity, and deliver a top-quality product." This is the language of substance. It has content and direction. It also stimulates controversy. People will disagree, particularly if the position taken affects their own power and place. So leading with substance requires maturity not only to tolerate others' aggressiveness but also to direct it to substantive issues.

Given that need, it is particularly unfortunate that many executives have been misled by experts who say that managing by ambiguity and indirection is the wave of the future. Indirection suggests what the speaker wants but veils it with polite and even deferential language. The result is that it encourages the acting out of psychodramas. Often the drama goes something like this. A subordinate is making a report and going in a direction the boss really doesn't like. Instead of saying "Those are terrible ideas. Here's what we should be doing," the well-trained manager asks courteously, "Have you considered the possibility of promoting the product with a premium instead of directly?" The question hardly invites the subordinate to get excited, defend his or her ideas, and tell the boss why the suggestion is a lousy idea. Instead, it just breeds more circumlocution, since the counterdefense in dealing with indirection is more indirection: "We gave that idea a lot of thought, and it has a lot going for it. But some new research suggests that premium promotion may fall a little short in getting the message across."

The cost of political games is the loss of creativity.

When a boss who is deeply (and probably unconsciously) angry manages by indirection, the effect can be really insidious—the kind of stuff that sets stomachs churning. For example, such managers often manipulate others by playing on their limited tolerance for anxiety. The psychodrama begins when the boss distances himself or herself from a subordinate. The subordinate, worried that something is wrong, tries to find out if he or she has caused some problem. The boss responds with reassuring words—and body language that says quite plainly, "You're in deep trouble!" Anxiety mounting, the subordinate begins to withdraw, till the boss, with exquisite timing, reverses direction and becomes genuinely supportive. As for the poor victim? Instead of feeling angry over this subtle oppression, he or she is grateful to the boss for relieving the awful burden of anxiety and diminished self-esteem. The end product is a subordinate who is less autonomous, more psychologically dependent, and more concerned with avoiding another identity-threatening episode than engaging in real work.

If this scenario were the whole story, organizations would produce a lot more stress than they do. The fact that it's not attests to how well men and women in organizations can defend themselves—not least by using their street smarts to play psychopolitical games themselves. Their gambit is to reverse the dependency flow, to make the boss need them more than they need the boss.

Playing this game means learning to be an organizational performer. Performers are adept at regulating the flow of information upward so that they're never faced with expectations they cannot meet. As long as their performance meets or exceeds the targets that have been set for them, the boss has little cause for scrutiny. But by the same token, the boss is also likely to understand very little about what subordinates are doing. The cost of this game is the demise of learning as well as the abandonment of any hope for creativity. Short-term results look good; the long-term is in jeopardy.

This analysis provokes a question: Is psychopolitics, or the victory of process over substance, the inevitable consequence of human nature, compounded by the complexity of living in a large, hierarchical organization? I think not. It's true that human beings learn political behavior in the nursery, in the competition for love and standing in the eyes of powerful parents and in childhood rivalries at school. But the politicization of work and human relationships is not an inevitable consequence of people being people. Rather, it goes hand in hand with reactive and defensive behavior.

And here, managers who want to stimulate real work and dampen political preoccupations can take a leaf from the book that sensible parents apply in raising their children. Such parents know that they cannot overcome the anxiety their children will inevitably feel as they develop and mature. Time cannot be made to stand still, nor can earlier satisfactions be sustained in the face of important developmental changes. So while these parents empathize with the children for whom they are responsible, they do not encourage them to wage an impossible war, a war that cannot be won on its own terms. Instead, like leaders, they learn to help the less powerful deal with life in different terms. They teach the lesson that substance is all, that the cultivation of talent is the genuine route to independence and maturity. They also teach their children that good human relations depend on what a person gives to the work at hand, not on what he or she takes.

Superior business performance requires senior executives who have overcome their own political anxieties and the need for total control over others. It also takes cadres of managers who are learning to do the same. For if managers continue to rise in organizations by playing psychopolitical games, and if their deepest propensities continue to lead them away from substance and the cultivation of talent toward politics and process, then there is little hope for real work and real competitiveness.

The real work of building canoes and cultivating the land is the sure and sane way to enhance morale in organizations. Exchanging beads in the Kula is merely an expressive reminder that those who contribute to the real work are the legitimate participants in the social satisfaction that accompanies true achievement. ⊟

Like wise parents, good managers teach that substance is all.

Reprint 89113

▶ Is our oldest human relations tool really a psychological piece of candy?

PRAISE REAPPRAISED

By Richard E. Farson

I am beginning to question the cherished idea that people enjoy being praised. I realize that I am in unfriendly territory because praise is perhaps the most widely used and thoroughly endorsed of all human relations techniques. Parents, businessmen, psychologists, teachers — everyone seems to believe in its value as a motivational tool, a reward, a way to establish good relationships.

But I wonder if praise accomplishes just what we think it does. Not that it does not have valuable functions (of which we are largely unaware), but I will bet our beliefs about its *value* are erroneous.

With considerable trepidation let me tentatively suggest:

— Praise is not only of limited and questionable value as a motivator, but may in fact be experienced as threatening.

— Rather than functioning as a bridge between people, it may actually serve to establish distance between them.

— Instead of reassuring a person as to his worth, praise may be an unconscious means of establishing the superiority of the praiser.

— Praise may constrict creativity rather than free it.

— Rather than opening the way to further contact, praise may be a means of terminating it.

Although we may be fooling ourselves as to what praise accomplishes, some of its functions

AUTHOR'S NOTE: The contributions of Toni Volcani, Harriet Washburn, and Jeanne Watson Eisenstadt to this article are gratefully acknowledged.

— such as maintaining distance, terminating contacts, establishing status or superiority — are in fact quite necessary and socially useful, even though we may prefer not to acknowledge these hidden benefits.

Definition

What is praise? We are all quick to distinguish praise from flattery, which has connotations of insincerity and expediency. For my purpose here, praise is any statement that makes a *positive* evaluation of an object, person, act, or event, and that contains very little supplementary information — for instance:

- "Nice work, you've done a fine job."
- "You're a good boy."
- "That painting of yours is excellent."

These are examples of praise — positive evaluations with little additional meaning.

On the other hand, a positive evaluation *plus* other information is not essentially, or merely, praise. A statement such as, "The reason I think you've done such a good job . . . ." or ,"How did you get that beautiful effect with ink alone?" invites a response and extends the encounter. Obviously such statements are more than praise and have different qualities and perhaps different results.

A simple definition or a simple analysis of praise is, of course, not possible. One must take into account the situation in which praise occurs, the history of the relationship one has with the other person, the attitudes that underlie the act of praise, and the motivations for it. Also, specific acts and techniques can never overcome the effects of one's basic attitudes toward others. Good relationships are dependent on good fundamental attitudes. And a good relationship can withstand many difficulties — even such difficulties as are brought on by praise.

Negative Aspects

What are the problems with praise?

First of all, the findings of scientific experiments on praise do not clearly demonstrate its value. Most of the studies done on this subject have compared praise with reproof or blame as motivational techniques. The results of these studies are mixed: in some cases praise was slightly more effective than reproof; in others, reproof was more effective than praise. In essence, all that can really be concluded from most research is that *some* response motivates people better than no response at all.

It has been demonstrated in psychological laboratories that we can shape human behavior by the use of rewards — symbols such as lights and bells which indicate that the subject is making correct responses or is gaining the approval of judges. But in the extremely complex situations of real life does praise work the same way? Does praise reward? After considerable observation I have come to the conclusion that it usually does not.

Watch people responding to praise. Don't they usually seem to be reacting with discomfort, uneasiness, and defensiveness? I have noticed that a very common response is a vague denial or derogation:

- "I really can't take the credit for it."

- "You're just saying that."

- "Well, *we* like it."

- "It was just luck."

- "I like yours, too."

- "Well, I do the best I can."

The one element these statements have in common is that they are all defensive reactions — efforts to cope with a difficult situation. Praise a house or garden and its owner hastens to point out its defects; praise an employee for a project and he is quick to play down his role in it. Under the stress of praise, some people often become uncomfortable, almost to the point of imitating the toe-digging reactions of small children. Apparently praise is something to be coped with, to be handled.

Reasons for Defensiveness

Why do people react to praise with defensiveness? Part of the reason may be that in praise there is threat — something one must defend against. After all, praise *is* an evaluation, and to be evaluated usually makes us uncomfortable. If we are weighed, we *may* be found wanting.

Most of us feel uncomfortable when we are negatively evaluated, so we tend to believe that positive evaluations should have the opposite effect, that they should be enhancing. Really, though, praise has many of the same basic problems and characteristics as do negative evaluations. Research indicates that *any* evaluation is likely to make people uncomfortable, defensive. Perhaps this is because, when you evaluate a person, you are often in some way trying to motivate him, to move him in a certain direction, to *change* him. Now while he himself may want to change, and while he may not like the person that he is, at the same time he *is* that person; his identity is very important, indeed essential, because it makes possible an answer to the question, "Who am I?" Bad or good he must hold onto his identity. For this reason the threat of change is one of the most fundamental and disquieting of psychological threats. So even though praise may only imply that one should change a bit in the direction one is already going, it *does* imply change, and therefore it may be almost as threatening as a negative evaluation.

Another reason why positive evaluation is discomforting lies in the fact that when a person praises us, it is clear that he is sitting in judgment. We become uneasy when we know someone is not only trying to change us but is continually judging us, grading us. In this situation, the absence of praise is especially threatening because we know that we are still being evaluated.

Often the change which praise asks one to make is not necessarily beneficial to the person being praised but will redound to the convenience, pleasure, or profit of the praiser. When we praise Tommy for making it to the bathroom in time, we are probably not so much delighted on Tommy's behalf as on our own; the change that complicated Tommy's life will make our own more convenient and pleasant. Much the same is true when we praise a salesman for neat call reports. Understandably, people feel threatened when they are being manipulated for another's benefit.

Our enthusiastic belief that praise is pleasing to people has resulted in its becoming a piece of psychological candy. We sugarcoat blame with praise, or use the "sandwich technique" whereby praise is followed by reproof, then again by praise. "I'm very pleased with your work, Fred," says the boss, "You're really getting the work out, *but* . . . ." Fred then gets the unhappy part of the story, the reprimand. The boss finishes up with, "Keep up the fine work," and Fred is shuttled out without quite knowing what hit him. This is also a favorite technique of parents and teachers. In fact, we have become so conditioned by its use from early childhood that when we are praised, we automatically get ready for the shock, the reproof.

Undoubtedly, the most threatening aspect of praise is the obligation it puts on us to be praiseworthy people. If we accept praise, if we really believe the best about ourselves, then we are under an obligation to behave accordingly. This is deeply frightening to us. For if we really believe it when we are told that we are competent, or intelligent, or beautiful, then we are continually on the spot to *be* competent, or intelligent, or beautiful, not only in the eyes of the person who praised us but, even worse, in our own eyes. The responsibility to be continually at our best, to live up to our talents and abilities, is perhaps our most difficult problem in living — and we naturally defend against it.

Issue of Credibility

It may be that there simply is no effective response to praise given in a face-to-face situation. Even saying "thank you" is not entirely satisfactory — although it may be the least defensive way of coping with the behavioral impasse which praise uniformly produces. Perhaps this is one reason why written praise may be somewhat easier to accept. We can savor it without having to invent a modest response.

Of course, part of the problem hinges on the issue of credibility. Can we really believe what the praiser seems to want us to believe? Written praise may be more credible and therefore more rewarding to us. It most certainly is when we discover a praising remark about us written in a letter not intended for us to see. But part of the credibility comes from within us. Are we psychologically prepared to accept the validity of comments which indicate our value? If you tell a person who strongly believes himself to be inadequate that he is in your opinion entirely adequate, then your statement is likely to be met with some resistance. The credibility of the praising remark has been determined by the person's internal needs to see himself in consistent ways.

Positive Functions

If praise is threatening to people for so many reasons, then why do we use it so often? Surely we do not want to retain in our repertoire responses that do not serve us in some functional way. What are the functions of praise? Why is it a conversational staple?

For one thing, people expect praise. We fish for compliments, subtly or openly. Why do we do this, if we don't really like praise? Probably because it is so important for each of us to feel valued by others. We hope that praise will make us feel that way. Sometimes it does. But because praise means so many things and exists in such complicated motivational contexts, its ability to reward us and indicate our value is questionable. Still, we invite it at the same time that we resist it. Perhaps in our other-directed society we have become so dependent on the approval of others that we must continually check just to make sure that we are not being devaluated.

For another thing, giving praise is easy to do. It makes conversation, and most of us have not enough energy, interest, or imagination to offer witty retorts, penetrating criticism, brilliant insights, or sensitive responses. We really do not want the burden of conversation to be that heavy anyway. Gross evaluations, like praise, are simpler and less demanding.

Then, too, praise, as we have seen, is a way of gaining status over another by establishing the fact that one is capable of sitting in judgment. Status is important to all of us, and though the person being evaluated may feel that the praise is threatening or diminishing, the praiser himself has increased his psychological size or, if he praises an inferior, has claimed or reinforced his status. It is interesting to note here that when the work of a high-status person is praised by a low-status person, this is often seen as presumptuous or even insulting. If a layman should tell Picasso, "You're a very good painter," he is not likely to be particularly well received. In order to be acceptable, he must give the praise in a way that respects the status difference.

Praise is also useful in maintaining the interpersonal distance. We talk a good deal about wanting to be close to people, but when you come right down to it, there really are very few people whom we want to be close to, or whom we admit to closeness with us. It is necessary to be able to maintain distance from people, to keep a little free space around ourselves — psychological elbowroom — especially in a society which fills our daily lives with so many contacts. In the search for techniques to establish distance between ourselves and others we find that praise is one of the most effective, simply because, when we evaluate people, we are not likely to gain emotional proximity to them. Compare the effects of praise with other behaviors, — for instance, listening to another or revealing your feelings to another, and see for yourself if praise doesn't tend to hold off, to separate, while the other behaviors tend to include, to embrace.

Control of Relationships

Praise also helps to keep relatively stable patterns of relationship between people. If organizations are to function smoothly, it is probably quite important that certain hierarchies or structures be maintained.

How does praise work toward this end? Let's take as an example a problem-solving committee meeting that includes the executive vice president at one end of the hierarchy and a new junior assistant at the other:

If the assistant comes up with the brightest and most useful idea, some way must be found to accept it without lowering the status of the vice president in the eyes of the group, thereby disturbing the group's stability. Intuitively, the vice president may say to the young assistant, "That's a very good idea, young man." This not-so-simple act of praise has greased the whole situation. Status has been maintained (because, as we remember, praise is a way of claiming status); the young man has been reminded of his place in the hierarchy; and the group is restored to comfortable equilibrium. Now the group can use the young man's idea without upsetting its psychological structure.

I am amazed to note how frequently we use praise as a sign that a conversation or interview is over. Listen and discover for yourself how many interpersonal transactions are ended with a positive evaluation. "It's good to talk with you" means "I've finished talking with you." And "You're doing fine; keep up the good work" communicates as well as any exit cue we have. For the busy parents to say to the child who has just offered her latest artistic creation, "Yes, Janie, that's a beautiful painting," may not better the relationship, but it will probably end the conversation. It is often tantamount to saying, "Go away; I'm busy right now." But of course we must have ways of doing just this, and praise is a very effective method.

So we see that by enabling us to terminate an encounter, by enabling us to keep a certain amount of psychological space between ourselves and others, by enabling us to maintain status — in short, to control our relationships — praise functions as one of the most important means by which we maintain consistent structure and equilibrium in any organization.

A Helpful Alternative

It is when we want to develop initiative, creativity, judgment, and problem-solving ability in people that praise fails us most. To liberate these qualities in people we need to rely on internal motivation. We need to make people feel that they are free of our control. We *may* need to establish a more equalitarian atmosphere, and sometimes we need to create a closeness with superiors. But if praise produces status differences, not equality; if it creates distance, not closeness; if it is felt as a threat, not as a reassurance; then how do you establish a free, accepting, yet close relationship that will encourage independent judgment, effective decisions, and creative actions?

There is much that is unknown about this, but from a variety of settings including psychotherapy, education, and business we are learning that perhaps the most important aspects of a helpful relationship are a person's ability to be *honest* and to *listen*. This sounds simple enough, but these behaviors are very seldom displayed in our relations with others.

Being Honest

This does not mean being brutally frank; it means showing some of yourself to another person, transparently exhibiting some of your own feelings and attitudes. This is not easy because from early childhood we have learned to play roles which mask our feelings, as if being honest about them would only hurt others and destroy relationships. Actually, it is the other way around; we mask our feelings so that we will not have too many close — and possibly burdensome — relationships. The inevitable consequence of exposing and sharing feelings is emotional closeness. But closeness, as rewarding as it sometimes can be, is often uncomfortable, unpredictable. Masking our feelings may result in some alienation and anxiety but also in a lot of superficial psychological comfort.

Hiding our feelings and playing roles help to make situations predictable. We want to know what we and other people are going to do and say. We want behavior to be patterned and familiar, not continually spontaneous and varied. Maybe this is necessary in order to have a society at all. Perhaps there is a limit to the amount of spontaneity, emotionality, honesty, and variation that can be tolerated by any social system.

Curiously, we are no more honest about the positive, loving feelings we have than about our feelings of annoyance, mistrust, resentment, or boredom. As a matter of fact, negative feelings usually are less difficult to express honestly than are positive feelings. For some reason it is easier for most people to be honest about their feelings of anger than it is for them to be honest about their feelings of caring and love. In either case, the times when one can risk vulnerability are perhaps life's richest moments — but are not often psychologically comfortable moments.

Empathic Listening

The other response which we find helpful in creating close relationships is to listen. This does not merely mean to wait for a person to finish talking, but to try to see how the world looks to this person and to communicate this understanding to him. This empathic, non-evaluative listening responds to the person's feelings as well as to his words; that is, to the total meaning of what he is trying to say. It implies no evaluation, no judgment, no agreement (or disagreement). It simply conveys an understanding of what the person is feeling and attempting to communicate; and his feelings and ideas are accepted as being valid for him, if not for the listener.

One reason we do not listen more, of course, is because it is too difficult. To see how difficult it is, try establishing in any group discussion the ground rule that no one may present his own view until he has first satisfied the person who

has just spoken that he fully comprehends what this person meant to communicate. That is, he must restate in his own words the total meaning of the message and obtain the person's agreement that this was indeed his message — that accurate listening did take place. In doing this we will find out that —

. . . it is extremely difficult to get one person to agree that he meant what another thought he meant;

. . . we usually fail in our attempts to understand;

. . . we typically spend our listening time preparing what we are going to say.

. . . when we do listen intently, we have a hard time remembering what it was that we were going to say, and when we do remember, we discover that it is a little off the subject;

. . . most argument and emotionality goes out of such a discussion;

. . . after a few minutes of this sort of "complete communication" we become rather weary.

It is also difficult to listen because if we allow ourselves to see the world through another's eyes and to fully understand his point of view, then we run the risk of changing ourselves, our own point of view. And, as previously indicated, change is something we try to avoid.

But at the times when we *do* want to develop creativity and self-confidence in others, when we *do* want to establish a close relationship in which the other person feels free "to be himself," then expressing our own feelings honestly and listening sensitively may be far more helpful than offering praise.

Try an Experiment

If you doubt the effects of praise outlined here, you might experiment a bit with it. Check for yourself. The next time you praise someone, see what sort of reaction you get:

√ Does he open up or does he become defensive, diffident, or uncomfortable?

√ Does he appear to want to continue talking or to terminate the talk?

√ Does he seem to be more motivated to work or does he seem less motivated?

Then check yourself too:

√ How do *you* feel when you receive praise?

√ What do you do and say in response to it?

√ How do you feel when you give praise?

√ What are you trying to accomplish by it?

Another experiment, perhaps even more telling, is to accept the praise offered to you just as it seems to be intended. That is, the next time some praise comes your way indicating that the praiser wants you to believe that you are competent, or good, or smart, or attractive, show him that you accept this evaluation of you by saying something like, "I guess you think I'm very competent," or, "You must think I'm a pretty good salesman." His reactions to this may indicate to you that his praise was intended to do much more than just convey that simple idea.

Let me sum up this way: It is questionable that praise is a fuel which motivates and stimulates people. On the other hand, praise is very useful indeed as a lubricant that keeps the wheels going around smoothly and predictably; we must have techniques like praise to keep our human relations in equilibrium.

Perhaps someday we will be able to look inward for evaluation rather than outward, to tolerate less order and equilibrium in our social organizations, and to enjoy increasing emotional closeness with greater numbers of people. But until that day praise will probably continue to serve us well in ways we seldom recognize.

Motivating the
Sales Force

GETTING THINGS DONE

Teamwork for Today's Selling

In many companies, the Willy Loman model has given way to coordination across product lines.

by Frank V. Cespedes, Stephen X. Doyle, and Robert J. Freedman

☐ Listen to this account manager, responsible for building sales and a close relationship with a key customer, describe a recent conversation with a colleague: "I called our district manager in Phoenix and explained that I was preparing an important proposal for this big account, and would he please help with the part of it having to do with an account location in his territory. He reluctantly agreed, but I haven't seen anything yet, and he hasn't returned my last two phone calls. With friends like that—"

This is how the district sales manager sees it: "I've got monthly numbers to meet with limited time and resources. And I don't get paid or recognized for helping someone else sell. So I don't."

☐ Now let's hear from the vice president of national accounts at a major telecommunications company: "We do about $3 million a year with Zembla [a large, diversified corporation] but that's peanuts compared with the potential. A big part of Zembla's strategy is their telecommunications network, which they've

sunk millions into over the past decade. Last week their information systems czar called me to complain about our salespeople in two regions. They were trying to sell a discount service to a couple of Zembla divisions, and they were succeeding. He said that this subverted his company's telecom strategy, which requires high utilization of Zembla's network to make it operate efficiently. Attempts to sell some of his people off that network were causing a lot of friction in his organization. And in ours too, I might add."

☐ Then there's the sales representative of a company where the proverbial 80% of revenue comes from

> "Until teamwork becomes a daily part of operations, the occasional pitch for it is only lip service."

20% of the customers. She sells equipment to some of those large accounts, while other salespeople in another sales force handle related supply items to the same accounts (among others). She says: "Many customers want to coordinate their purchases of equipment and supplies because of the impact they have on their production processes. But equipment sales are usually higher priced transactions than supply sales, occur much less often, and involve contact with more people from more functions in the customer's organization. So you have more sales calls and a longer selling cycle, as well as different delivery and service requirements after the sale is made. I meet a lot with my supply brethren because, while we share all of our accounts, what's often not shared or clear are our individual goals."

☐ A sales manager comments on his company's recent annual sales meeting: "Great resort, wonderful food, and the weather was terrific. Our senior VP of sales and marketing made his annual speech on teamwork. But that's not enough. Until teamwork becomes a daily part of operations, the occasional pitch for it is only lip service."

For many companies in the past two decades, selling has changed dramatically. Traditionally it was the vocation of a single energetic, persistent individual—"a man way out there in the blue, riding on a smile and a shoeshine," in Arthur Miller's memorable words. Now selling is often the province of a team composed of men and women who must coordinate their efforts across product lines (the products often made by different divisions and sold from different locations) to customers that require an integrated approach. Even when there is no formal sales team,

Frank V. Cespedes is an assistant professor at the Harvard Business School, where he teaches marketing. Stephen X. Doyle is president of SXD Associates, a sales management consulting firm. Robert J. Freedman is a vice president at TPF&C, where he specializes in sales and executive compensation.

moreover, it's often necessary to coordinate—as the vignettes at the start of this article show.

Mergers, acquisitions, and other changes in the business environment are forcing vendors in many industries to put greater emphasis on large customers with equally large and complex purchasing requirements. Conventional supermarkets, for example, accounted for about 75% of U.S. retail food sales in 1980. They will take in an estimated 25%

> # Vendors increasingly have big customers with big, complex purchasing requirements.

in 1990; "super stores," "combination stores," and "warehouse stores" will account for most remaining sales. These chains possess the buying power (backed by sophisticated information systems) they need to insist on better service, lower prices, and a coordinated approach from their vendors, many of whom sell them multiple products through different sales forces.

Similar trends are evident in many industrial goods categories, where just-in-time inventory systems make customers aware of any discrepancies in prices, terms and conditions, delivery, or timely attention by vendors' salespeople in many buying locations. Internationally, the emergence of more multinational, even global customers places similar demands on many sales organizations—with distance, currency variations, and cultural differences in the vendor's sales force adding complications to the administration of these important shared accounts.

In these situations, selling depends on the vendor's ability to marshal its resources effectively across a range of buying locations, buying influences, product lines, and internal organizational boundaries. Coordination in these shared-account situations affects the company's

expense-to-revenue ratio, ability to retain current business or develop new business at these accounts, and sales force morale and management. Yet, as the comments by salespeople indicate, coordination is not easy.

At four sellers of industrial goods we studied, only 11% of the salespeople involved in shared accounts were located in the same building, while 43% were in different sales districts and 7% in different countries. Of course, this dispersion erects time, expense, and scheduling barriers to coordination, and the problem is likely to get worse as many customers become more multinational in scope. Further, although development work on major accounts often takes years, one-quarter of the salespeople had been in their account positions less than five years. "It takes time to develop good working relationships on an account team," one sales manager explained, but account continuity is a recurring issue at these and many other companies.

In interviews, salespeople repeatedly cited more communication as the one thing that could most improve teamwork on shared accounts. In view of the distances and compensation involved, however, improving communication—especially the preferred mode, meetings—would raise these companies' marketing expense-to-revenue ratios to unacceptable levels. There is no doubt that a coordinated sales approach can be expensive. So, like any other expensive business resource, it should be employed where it will yield the highest returns.

Because the need for sales coordination depends on the complexity of the account, moreover, both large and small vendors face these issues. Large companies may enjoy scale advantages over the smaller competition, but they often have more products to sell and more layers in their sales and marketing hierarchies, making coordination among their salespeople difficult.

Smaller companies may have less bureaucracy than the big competition, but with fewer products and fewer resources they often base their marketing strategies on superior responsiveness to customers via

customized marketing programs. Hence, this important source of competitive advantage for the smaller vendor raises the threshold of coordination required. Actually, our research showed that despite significant size differences among the various companies that we studied, the number of salespeople who must work together in shared accounts remained about the same at each company.

Our data and experience indicate three areas that are most important in sales coordination: compensation systems, the goal-setting process, and staffing and training issues that arise when shared accounts are an integral part of sales strategy.

Compensation systems

In sales management, you won't get what you don't pay for. One salesperson put it this way: "Teamwork reflects many elements. However, compensation is a foundation. An individual's belief that he or she is paid fairly spurs belief in the team concept."

Many companies have three types of teamwork situations:

1. Joint efforts on behalf of certain national or international accounts, in which all team members work exclusively with these accounts.

2. Headquarters national account managers (NAMs) or account executives coordinate with field sales reps; the NAM is dedicated to one or two accounts, but these accounts are among dozens or even hundreds that field sales representatives call on.

3. District sales managers' efforts affect important accounts that cut across sales district lines, but performance evaluations are based on intradistrict results.

To encourage the kind of teamwork required, a different compensation system may be appropriate for each type of sales rep and account situation. Flexibility is the key, and this often means complexity. Yet in big-account situations, many companies design compensation plans according to "keep it simple, stupid" criteria, however complex the sales tasks are. Top management then ignores important differences tied to account assignments and often re-

About Our Research

In gathering material for this article, we concentrated on four companies with sizable sales forces selling industrial goods. We administered a comprehensive questionnaire, which 835 people completed. About two-thirds were sales representatives and one-third, sales managers. About half of the group had worked in sales for more than a decade.

The perspectives in this article also reflect many conversations with sales managers, marketing managers, field sales representatives, and senior executives at these and other companies.

wards selling activity that neglects coordination at the customer.

If there are many salespeople calling on key accounts and teamwork is important, then a bonus based on total account sales often makes more sense than traditional, individually oriented incentive arrangements. Interep is the nation's largest radio "rep" firm; its salespeople in major U.S. cities call on ad agencies and advertisers to sell time on the more than 3,000 radio stations it represents. To avoid bureaucracy and maintain an entrepreneurial spirit, Interep's chairman, Ralph Guild, has spread the company's sales efforts among six different sales forces.

Mergers among big advertisers and ad agencies, however, have made customers increasingly receptive to a rep firm that can act as a coordinated supplier across various radio markets for different product categories. In response, Interep uses a team approach to selling that cuts across each sales force. A prime element is the compensation system. Unlike the plans at most other rep firms, where incentives are staunchly "Lone Ranger" in design, Interep has salespeople with shared-account responsibilities participate in a bonus pool based on the particular account's sales volume. The approach

has been effective: Interep's sales are growing faster than the industry's, and according to market surveys, ad agencies generally view Interep as more responsive than competitors.

Another important compensation issue is the time frame employed. Sales efforts at big accounts often take months, sometimes years, to pan out. But compensation plans usually tie incentives to quarterly or annual snapshots of performance. The usual result, as one salesperson acknowledged, is this: "Because our compensation plan is short-term oriented, I put my efforts where there are short-term benefits. Also, many short-term sales goals can be met with a minimum of teamwork; the longer term results require the hassle of working with lots of other people." Bonuses for multiple-year performance, or for qualitative objectives like building relationships with certain account decision makers, can encourage team effort.

Sharing of sales credit is a nettlesome issue. Surveys of major account sales programs show that only a minority use credit splitting to help coordinate NAMs and field sales reps.[1] In shared accounts, split credits are often better than mutually exclusive credit decisions.

But not always. One sales rep noted how a common attitude toward split credits can fuel resentment and block teamwork: "Most salespeople feel that when the split is 50/50, they're losing 50% instead of gaining 50% of the incentive pay. A lot of time and energy is wasted arguing over splits."

Actually, a company can give full credit to those involved and still not (as many managers fear) pay twice for the same sale. The key is having a good understanding of the sales tasks involved and an information system capable of tracking performance so that shared sales volume can be taken into account when setting objectives. Consider an example: two salespeople last year sold about $500,000 each to individual accounts and about $500,000 to shared accounts. Their combined sales amounted to about $1.5 million. Two approaches to goal setting and credits are possible:

□ The employer sets targets and bonuses so that each person receives $25,000 for $750,000 in sales, with credit from shared account sales split 50/50. If each sells $500,000 in individual sales and $500,000 to shared accounts, each makes the $750,000 target and gets a bonus.
□ The employer pays a $25,000 bonus for $1 million of sales with all shared-account volume double counted and fully credited to both people. Each salesperson must then rely on team effort for about 50% of target sales, but each also receives full credit for team sales.

A participant in the first plan may reason that an incremental $250,000 in individual sales (perhaps developed at the expense of time devoted to the more complicated joint sales effort) could reach the $750,000 target. Consequently, he or she might decide to concentrate on individually assigned accounts, encourage the colleague to continue to work hard on the team accounts, and hope to gather those half-credit sales with little or no effort. Coordination and major account penetration are likely to suffer. Under the second plan, there is at least no compensation barrier to expenditure of effort on the more labor-intensive team sales.

Compensation alone won't harness teamwork if other control systems are out of kilter. But ill-defined compensation plans can thwart teamwork even when other control systems support coordination.

Setting and meeting goals

Compensation means money. A less expensive way to foster teamwork is by clarifying goals – defining individual salespeople's main responsibilities and desired accomplishments (like opening new accounts, maximizing sales from existing accounts, and launching new products). When goals are unclear, selling can be frustrating because salespeople cannot know where they stand in relation to some standard. Good performance may appear then to be a random occurrence, independent of effort. This confusion can

1. Gary Tubridy, "How to Pay National Account Managers," *Sales & Marketing Management*, January 13, 1986, p.52.

discourage effort, especially in those tasks that require working with other people.

Disseminating information about company strategy helps to clarify sales goals and the effort top management wants. Yet few companies regularly pass on information to the sales force about the company's objectives in its various market segments. Many so-called "strategic plans" do not make meaningful reference to the sales force's role in implementing strategy. Instead, the

> ## A close fit of sales goals with strategic goals, clearly understood, is essential.

goals coming out of senior executive negotiations are usually kept secret because of fear that wide dissemination would unwittingly include competitors.

A strategy that does not imply certain behavior by the sales force, however, is often no strategy; it's merely an interesting idea. In the context of sales teamwork, moreover, competitive cost data are usually not what salespeople want; they need information about the company's goals in the marketplace, the nature of its potential competitive advantage, and their role in achieving those goals. Withholding this information is counterproductive. If salespeople are not selling in accordance with corporate goals, withholding information about strategy will not help; and if salespeople *are* selling in accordance with corporate goals, competitors will learn about them anyway.

One company we studied makes automatic testing equipment that is often bought to function as part of a total quality-control system at customer locations. Hence extensive customization for customers' production processes and information networks is necessary. These products are technologically dynamic and complex, demanding comprehensive product knowledge on sales-

people's part. So the sales force is divided into product-oriented units.

The company holds semiannual sales meetings where the importance of integrated selling strategies is high on the agenda and where, in small groups, salespeople and senior executives talk about joint sales work and cross-selling activities on specific accounts. Top management considers these sessions as both an important input and output of strategic planning in a business where product development costs and an increasingly multinational customer base make account selection and incremental sales to major customers a key aspect of strategy.

In situations like this, where goal clarity and information about those goals are intertwined, managers might use the following checklist of questions to perform a quick audit of sales teamwork:

1. Do the goals spelled out to salespeople fit the company's strategic objectives? The compensation plan? One U.S. company, responding to the increasing globalization of its markets, began joint ventures with Japanese and German companies, realigned its product line and manufacturing operations at great cost, and established an ambitious "global account management" program. Quotas for the U.S. sales force, however, continued to focus on domestic accounts, and commissions were tied to domestic deliveries. Sales goals and corporate objectives were out of sync. Sometimes U.S. sales reps even tried to talk customers with foreign operations out of buying a product from one of the company's overseas operations! The frequent result: no sale at all.

2. Does the sales force understand the goals? Attention must be paid to "recommunicating" goals regularly —not least because the makeup of the sales force is always changing.

At IBM, account planning sessions spanning three to five days and often involving as many as 50 people have long been standard features of big-account management. The sales force discusses each account's business conditions and decision-making processes, and the staff con-

cerned reviews all account applications, installations, and maintenance issues. The chief objective is an updated account plan for sales personnel.

Another goal is to acquaint people with the status of the account, including people in support roles. The impact on their morale and on the coordination of their efforts is an often overlooked, but crucial, aspect of sales teamwork. At one large medical equipment supplier, fast delivery is an important aspect of service to major hospital accounts. So account meetings include the truck drivers who regularly deliver to these accounts. "Knowing the warehouse," they can often make the difference in expediting a key customer's order.

3. Are the goals measurable? Do the sales managers reinforce them? In most busy organizations, "that which is not measured does not happen," as one sales manager sardonically noted. Some companies respond to the more protracted and more complicated nature of shared-account sales by relaxing or ignoring measures. In such cases, the field salespeople often feel "We do the work, while the major account managers play golf and get the glory." It is precisely *because* shared-account sales demand sustained attention that measures are important. Without them, the pull in most sales organizations is toward the shorter term, individually assigned accounts.

Sales volume is only one measure of shared-account performance. Profitability, cross-selling, or new product introductions are often more appropriate measures, depending on the vendor's strategy.

Qualitative as well as quantitative measures may figure in evaluation of performance. At many investment banks, for example, a common source of data for evaluating individual performance at bonus time is input from colleagues via cross-evaluation surveys of collaborators on various deals. Account executives and product specialists may evaluate each other on certain criteria, including the other's contribution in marketing and service efforts for clients. These surveys keep account people sensitive to the coordi-

"Hold it, Al...if we're going to talk marketing, I'm going to switch to my marketing hat."

nation requirements of their jobs and keep managers aware of potential problems.[2]

Staffing and training

"I've worked alone 14 years in this territory," one field sales rep said, "and I prefer an 'I'll call you, don't call me' relationship with team players." A revamped compensation plan and an effective goal-setting procedure may change her attitude, but the odds are against it.

Teamwork in sales, as in sports and many other endeavors, is the sum of individual efforts working cooperatively toward a common goal. And just as most ballplayers play better in some conditions than they do in others, some hitting right-handed pitchers better and some left-handers, so do different salespeople perform better in some circumstances than in others. This has implications for account staffing. The sales rep we quoted should not be required or even asked to work in team-selling situations. The "don't

call me, I'll call you" attitude won't help and may hurt in these circumstances. As long as her performance is acceptable, she should continue where she is.

A team process for recruiting is helpful for spotting such loners. At many companies, including Digital Equipment, interviews with team members are a crucial part of the hiring procedure. A team process is also useful for acquainting a prospect with account characteristics and corporate goals.

A perennial question for many companies that have key-account sales programs is whether to fill vacancies internally or hire externally. Most of the companies we looked at preferred to promote from within on the ground that understanding of the organization is more important and useful than general sales experience or even industry familiarity picked up at another vendor. Why? One reason is that shared-account programs place salespeople in positions where they have little authority over others

who affect their performance on accounts. In such a situation, things get done through persuasion (helped by an informal reckoning of personal debits and credits), a knowledge of how the organization sets budgets and allocates resources, and a network of relationships cultivated over time. Outsiders, however knowledgeable and competent, are at a disadvantage in these areas.

At one company, a vendor of medical supplies, the account executive is called the "quarterback" of the company's resources for an account, and managers use the metaphor of a lens to describe the account manager's job: to bring into focus for a key account the company's resources in areas ranging from R&D and product development to distribution and customer service. Effective performance in this role calls for account executives who know internal systems as well as they know their ac-

2. Robert G. Eccles and Dwight B. Crane, *Doing Deals: Investment Banks at Work* (Boston: Harvard Business School Press, 1988).

counts' buying processes and purchase criteria.

As sales tasks change, sales training should change too. In shared-account situations, product knowledge and generic selling skills (e.g., presentation expertise and time management) remain important, but the coordination requirements make other skills necessary as well. In major-account programs, salespeople usually work across product lines, often across sales forces and, increasingly, across country sales organizations that reflect different national cultures. Furthermore, line authority in these situations is often ephemeral, since coordinators, like NAMs and account executives, often have dotted-line relationships with other sales personnel. Team building is a crucial part of sales competence in these situations.

Yet, as one sales rep (echoing many others) noted to us, "All sales training I've ever seen in my company stresses development of individual skills, not teamwork. As a result, delegating responsibility and working with and through others are seen as weaknesses, not strengths, in our sales force."

Attention to team training is particularly important in companies with multiple sales forces, especially when they speak different technical or trade languages. Exposure to the other sales force's product line in training sessions can help. Mixed sales meetings encourage idea sharing across district or product lines and, equally important, build acquaintances among individuals who can later call on one another during an account crisis or opportunity.

A barrier to such training efforts is often not the money involved but the source of the money. Sales training is a significant expenditure at most companies—and, because the numbers usually do not reflect the cost of salespeople's time out of the field, a usually underestimated expenditure. But training budgets are often set according to district results or the performance of a particular

sales group. The local managers who set the budgets naturally focus training on specific sales opportunities; they have little incentive to devote training to team efforts. A task for executives at many companies is to determine whether the method they use to apportion expenditures on sales training supports a goal of better sales coordination.

Situational teamwork

How a company thinks about improving sales coordination depends to a large extent on its products and the way it sells. Look at two organizations we studied, Company X, a supplier of automatic testing equipment, and Company Y, which sells business equipment and supplies.

While both handle large accounts where teamwork is essential, X sells technically complex and high unit-priced products, and Y sells technically simple products with lower unit prices. X has a small sales force and Y a large one. X's salespeople (mostly engineers) deal with long selling cycles and complex customer decision-making processes, while Y's salespeople (most without technical backgrounds) encounter shorter selling cycles and a more easily identifiable set of decision makers at their accounts. X's salespeople tend to place less emphasis on money (compensation systems, sales contests) and measurements (formal performance evaluation criteria) as control and coordination mechanisms than on "people issues" (relationships within the sales group and sales supervisors' skills). Y's salespeople tend to stress money and measurements as the key factors affecting teamwork.

These differences seem tied to the tasks facing salespeople at these companies and coincide with others' observations about the way task complexity affects the nature of the selling effort required.[3] The more complex the selling task, the more information must be exchanged between vendor and customer and the more information passed around among the vendor's salespeople working on a common account. Especially in technical sales situations, moreover, this information must be

coordinated among people trained in certain core disciplines as well as in sales techniques. At the other extreme is the salesperson with the simple product whose mandate is a simple "go out and sell." Less information has to be transmitted between buyer and seller and among salespeople.

One inference to be drawn is that in complex sales tasks the initial selection of salespeople is more important. The technical skills required are expensive to obtain and keep honed through training; and the coordination skills necessary are more dependent on individual relationships. Where the sales task is less complex, however, requiring less information to be understood and communicated, "systems solutions" to coordination (mechanisms like compensation and measurement systems) are potentially more appropriate and respected by the sales force.

Organizations are often diligent in setting budgets, creating organization charts, and establishing other types of formal control systems. But they are often less attentive to the

> While most top managers support teamwork, their organizations don't focus on team effectiveness.

crucial but "softer" aspects of sales management. Sales managers in the companies we studied overwhelmingly stressed formal control systems (like compensation and quota-setting mechanisms) in their coordination efforts, while salespeople favored processes (like relationships with other salespeople and long-established company norms that aid or inhibit coordination). Sales managers are no doubt more com-

Authors' note: We thank Professor Benson P. Shapiro of the Harvard Business School for his helpful comments on an early draft of this article.

3. Benson P. Shapiro, "Manage the Customer, Not Just the Sales Force," HBR September-October 1974, p. 127; and Barton A. Weitz, "Effectiveness in Sales Interactions: A Contingency Framework," Journal of Marketing, Winter 1981, p. 85.

fortable with formal systems; they are easier to install and measure than initiatives aimed at nurturing process in the sales environment—and so easier to justify at budget-setting sessions. But in many situations, managers may be trying to address what salespeople perceive as interpersonal issues in teamwork with administrative "solutions."

While most top managers support teamwork, very few organizations actually focus on team effectiveness, and few managers get the process going on their own without the organization's support. As one sales executive commented, "Sales teamwork is ultimately a by-product of the organization and has to come from the top down. People in the trenches can be team players, but they need encouragement and incentives. Preaching teamwork won't work as long as senior managers' attitude toward the sales force remains at the carrot-and-stick level."

In seeking to make a sales organization more effective, however, it's important for management to keep aware of a key distinction: coordination doesn't necessarily mean consensus. That is, a team shouldn't approximate the dictionary definition of "two or more beasts of burden harnessed together." Years ago in *The Organization Man*, William Whyte skewered a certain pseudo teamwork that has a numbing and leveling effect on individual performance, creativity, and expression—qualities that are always vital in effective sales and marketing. But Whyte also missed the point: there are so many tasks in business that can only be carried on through groups. A sales manager with 20 years of experience put it this way: "You cannot legislate teamwork. It's an attitude that comes over the long term, and it's essential in a well-run sales organization. Despite this, there still needs to be plenty of room for individual success and achievement. Otherwise, teamwork becomes an amorphous concept that can lead a group to underachieve in harmony." Our suggestions can mean increased rewards for both the company and the individual salesperson.

Reprint 89205

What counts most in motivating your sales force?

The nature of the sales task has more to do with motivation than personality, compensation plan, or quality of management

*Stephen X. Doyle and
Benson P. Shapiro*

Two salespeople with about the same need to achieve, the same kind of compensation plan, and the same quality of management could perform differently. The thing that would make the difference, these authors have found, is the nature of the selling task itself. In studying the sales systems of four different companies, two with a clearly defined sales task and two without, the authors discovered that salespeople work longer hours on their job when the task is clear—when they see a positive and firm relationship between their effort and results. The authors also found that the other motivating factors have differing influences on motivation as well. Working with the rankings of the four motivating factors, managers can design sales systems that will produce the maximum motivation for that sales task. Fortunately, even in industries where the sales task is necessarily unclear, such as in transportation services companies, managers can redesign it so that salespeople can get the feedback they need on their individual performance to fuel their willingness to work.

Stephen X. Doyle received his doctorate from the Harvard Business School in 1976 and is president of SXD Associates, a management consulting firm in Great Neck, New York. Benson P. Shapiro is professor of business administration at the Harvard Business School.

Reprint 80305

For decades the difficulty of motivating salespeople has been frustrating sales and marketing managers. To the most effective ones, two things are clear: one, the job is difficult; two, there is no one simple solution. Believing that "good salespeople are born, not made," many managers recognize that recruiting is important. Others holding that "if you pay for performance, you'll get it" believe that incentive compensation produces motivation. The more successful sales executives recognize that motivation is largely a result of a combination of effective recruiting practices, sensible pay plans, and good management. What else may be involved has been an open question.

Previous studies on employee motivation clearly demonstrate that a variety of factors (rewards, supervision, goals, and so forth) shape and guide how well people work.[1] From a sales manager's point of view, then, two questions are paramount:

1. Which factors have the most influence on motivation of salespeople?

2. What are the implications for management action and decision making?

To answer the first question, we recently conducted a study to determine how much a person's personality and incentive pay determine level of motivation. Then, because we believed from prior experience that task clarity, another variable, has a pronounced effect on salesperson motivation, we included it in our study as well. Finally, we looked

Authors' note: This study was funded by the Associates of the Harvard Business School and the Western Electric Fund. The authors appreciate the generous support of these organizations.

1. For a good summary of the area, see Orville C. Walker, Jr., Gilbert A. Churchill, and Neil M. Ford, "Motivation and Performance in Industrial Selling: Present Knowledge and Needed Research," *Journal of Marketing Research*, vol. XIV, May 1977, p. 156.

Methodology

In our research of the motivating factors, we used multiple measures such as structural questionnaires, open-ended interviews, and field visits with sales representatives. These. were designed to gather information on the relationships among the independent variables – design of the sales pay plan, quality of supervision, nature of the selling task – and the dependent variables, motivation and performance.

We used four measures to assess motivation and performance. The first was actual hours per week spent selling and in sales-related activities. The second was hours spent in the evening or on weekends in job-related activities. The third was the percent increase or decrease in units sold and revenues compared to the same period the previous year. The fourth and last measure was the strength of the sales representative's expectations.[†]

This article uses the first measure (hours spent per week selling or in sales-related activities) to assess levels of motivation. The first and second measures correlate highly at the .91 level and are therefore interchange-able. We could not report on the revenue increases or decreases because of confidentiality agreements. Also revenue increases and decreases were the result of other factors such as changes in the economy and in marketing programs. Our primary purpose was to measure salesperson motivation and effort as precisely and accurately as possible. We believe that the time a salesperson spends on selling and sales-related activities is a clear and precise measure of motivation.

The final form of the questionnaire contained a total of 68 questions. Most of the key variables were measured by at least two items. In an effort to establish reliability, we administered a retest to a number of sales representatives from a service organization. Using a three-week time spread between the first and second test, we then examined the pairs of questionnaires, and the reliability coefficient indicated no significant variation. We also spent three consecutive days each calling on diverse customers with two sales representatives from each of the four participating companies.

Authors' note: The questionnaire was designed and produced with help from a number of different sources, including: (1) Survey Research Center, Institute for Social Research, University of Michigan; (2) Edwards Personal Preference Schedule; (3) Internal-External (I-E) Scale*; and (4) Jay W. Lorsch and John J. Morse, *Organizations & Their Members: A Contingency Approach* (New York: Harper & Row, 1974), methodological appendix.

*See J.B. Rotter, "Generalized Expectancies for Internal Versus External Control of Reinforcement," *Psychological Monographs*, 1966, vol. 80, (1), p.1.

†R.L. Oliver, "Expectancy Theory Predictions of Salesmen's Performance," *Journal of Marketing Research*, August 1974, p. 243.

at the impact of good management. (We describe the methodology in the accompanying ruled insert.)

In our research, we conducted in-depth interviews with salespeople and their managers, analyzed a questionnaire filled out by more than 200 salespeople in four different organizations, and observed some actual sales calls.

The four participating companies provide a broad sampling of current sales management practices. Two of the companies sell business products and two sell transportation services; all four are industry leaders. Of the business products companies, one manufactures and sells minicomputers; the other, office equipment. The transportation companies specialize in air freight serving domestic and inter-national markets. One transportation services company and one business products company pay salespeople a straight salary. The other two companies use incentive plans.

Our results are clear. The most important determinants of motivation are (1) the nature of the task, (2) the personality, particularly the strength of the salesperson's need for achievement, and (3) the type of compensation plan. Unfortunately, our measurement of the fourth determinant, the quality of management, is not precise enough for us to say any more than that field supervision is important. We believe, however, that if a company's management is not far outside the normal range in quality, its effect on motivation is below that of task clarity and salesperson personality. *Exhibit I* shows the four factors ranked in order of their importance. (The ranking is a result of a statistical analysis that measured independently each factor's ability to motivate salespeople.)[2]

Before discussing in more detail the impact each variable has on motivation and performance, we'd like to describe more fully exactly why motivating salespeople is such an enormous problem. Understanding the salesperson's role is key.

Salespeople vary greatly in what they do as well as what they are expected to do.[3] Some, alone and unsupervised, sell simple products such as books and magazines door to door. Others, working as a team, sell complex technical products such as power plants and aircraft. For some salespeople the eventual purchase of their product is far removed from their "sale." For example, when detail people who do missionary selling of pharmaceutical drugs leave the physician's office, it is difficult for anyone, perhaps even the physician, to know if a sale was made. Only through a postaudit of prescriptions is it possible to identify the outcome.

The salespeople we are concerned with here are full-time professionals who generally sell to business and industry, not to consumers. We believe, however, that our findings are generally applicable even to part-time salespeople selling door to door.

The salesperson we are interested in:

> Meets rejection by influential executives many times a week.

(If four companies are vying for a particular order, three salespeople will be turned down and, in a sense, personally rejected.)

2. N.H. Nie, C.H. Hull, J.G. Jenkins, K. Steinbrenner, and D.H. Kent, *Statistical Package for the Social Sciences*, 2nd ed. (New York: McGraw-Hill, 1975), p. 404.

3. See, for example, Gilbert A. Churchill, Neil M. Ford, and Orville C. Walker, Jr., "Organizational Climate and Job Satisfaction in the Sales Force," *Journal of Marketing Research*, vol. XIII, November 1976, p. 323.

> Works independently, away from direct supervision, for long periods.

> Works alone, away from the community of people.

> Functions at a high energy level all day, every day.

> Makes quick, accurate assessments of many new business situations and people on a regular basis.

> Appreciates and is constantly sensitive to the personal and organizational needs of others.

> Seems "bigger than life" in order to sell to the customer and make a positive, lasting impression.

> Balances the needs of a demanding customer with the sometimes unresponsive abilities and nature of the company.

(At times it is difficult for the salesperson to identify the "antagonist." Sometimes it is a purchasing agent or an executive in the buying company, and sometimes it seems to be the shipping manager in the salesperson's own company.)

It is no wonder that salespeople are difficult to motivate. Now let's take a closer look at the four factors necessary for a motivated sales system, and then we'll explore the implications for action.

A clear sales task

Obviously, the nature of selling differs from one company to another. For example, a pharmaceutical detail person calling on physicians has a very different job from an account executive selling apparel or an account manager selling materials-handling systems. We can categorize what people do in vastly different sales jobs according to how clear their tasks are. Task clarity is the degree to which there is a clear and positive relationship between exerting effort and attaining results. In sales, this characteristic varies from one selling job to another, depending on two major conditions: (1) the time span of performance feedback and (2) the degree that one can accurately determine the individual results of salespeople.

Our research shows that these components of task clarity can be accurately determined. In the participating companies, the selling jobs displayed strong differences, which are outlined in Exhibit II (see page 58).

Exhibit I
The four motivating factors in order of importance*

Motivating factor	Description	Percent variation explained by the factor
Task	Design of the sales job itself	33.6%
Personality	Strength of the salesperson's need for achievement	21.2
Compensation	Design of the program by which salespeople are paid	11.6
Quality of management	Method of field sales supervision	–

*The ability to motivate is expressed by the percent variation explained by each factor.
Note: Data in all exhibits represent averages.

We determined the conditions of the sales tasks in the four companies from the comments of managers and our own assessments, which correspond, furthermore, to the individual assessments of the salespeople. For example, a salesperson in a business products company with a clear task comments:

"It is quite easy to describe our job. We go by the numbers; in fact, we have numbers for everything. Our performance goals are very clear. Also on Friday afternoon we get a printout that gives feedback on our results. It is very easy to see the relationship between my effort and results. My territory stays the same for a year; I get frequent updates about new orders and reorders. In fact, I just told some trainees that attaining sales goals is not difficult as long as they plan and are willing to exert some effort."

A transportation services salesperson with an unclear task describes her job much differently: "Sure we get credited sales reports, but they are only 50% to 60% accurate. The accounting office has admitted that they have trouble crediting revenue to the person who produced it. Even though I understand their problem, it makes it tough on us in terms of accurately pinpointing what we produce. The truth is that our objective measures, such as shipment counts, are not accurate at the district level. I guess you could say no one really knows how well his or her territory is doing at any given time."

This salesperson's district sales manager supported her comments. He stated that field sales reports are inaccurate because of the difficulty in crediting the revenue from millions of shipments, averaging less than $50 per shipment, to the salesperson involved in the sale. For example, each week a large manufacturer of microprocessors located in the Santa Clara Valley of California ships and receives hundreds of air freight parcels to customers all over the United States. The sale—the manufacturer's decision

Exhibit II
Task clarity of sales job in four companies

Condition determining task clarity	Business products organizations	Transportation services organizations
Time span of performance feedback	Short – one day to one week	Long – one to three months
Degree that individual results can be accurately measured	High	Low to moderate
Task clarity	High	Low

to use air freight as well as a specific air transportation company—may have been made in the Santa Clara Valley or in various destination cities. The individual salesperson, therefore, has no way of knowing whether the revenue increases in his or her territory were caused by a colleague in a distant city.

As a result regional and district revenue reports do not reflect individuals' efforts. Also, because of the nature of the sales task, fewer than 7% of the sales calls generate new business. The most tangible evidence of new business is an oral or written commitment on the part of the shipper to use the services of the company at some future time.

Our study shows that the clarity of the sales task is strongly related to on-the-job performance and effort. Motivation and effort in the clear sales task of the two business products organizations are substantially greater than in the relatively unclear sales task of the transportation services companies (see A in Exhibit III). If a sales task is unclear, selling can be frustrating. In such a situation, the salesperson will not know where he or she stands and will not be able to pinpoint the results of his or her own efforts. Good performance seems to be a random occurrence in no way related to effort. This lack of connection is discouraging and dampens the pride that might otherwise come from accomplishment.

People who need to achieve

Managers know intuitively that personality differences are an important determinant of on-the-job performance, and a number of studies confirm their feelings.[4] Our study was aimed at finding out how differences in need for achievement, as described by David McClelland, influence the motivation of sales representatives.[5] McClelland has characterized the person with a high need to achieve as one who likes to take responsibility for solving problems, sets

moderate achievement goals, takes calculated risks, desires feedback on performance, and is likely to find selling rewarding and challenging.

We found that the degree of a person's need for achievement is directly related to sales force motivation (see B in Exhibit III). As need for achievement increases, so do effort and motivation. In fact, as a group, the motivation of those with higher achievement needs is 13% greater than those with lower needs.

The total group of 204 salespeople scored relatively high on need for achievement. There are two probable explanations for this. First, as McClelland states, people who have a high need for achievement tend to gravitate toward sales jobs. Second, the participating companies' selection and hiring processes use multiple interviews and emphasize a record of past accomplishments that could show a high need to achieve. (Implicitly, all the companies were trying to recruit people with a high need to achieve.) A regional sales manager in one of the business products companies comments:

"Our motivational plan is built around goals, evaluation, and hiring the right people. It is not unusual for an applicant to visit our office six or seven times before a hiring decision is made. I want to get to know each person as thoroughly as possible before I make a commitment. During these interviews I look for a strong record of accomplishment [in school, business, or social settings] and indications that the applicant is very results oriented."

4. David Mayer and Herbert M. Greenberg, "What Makes a Good Salesman," HBR July-August 1964, p. 119; E.E. Ghiselli, The Validity of Occupational Aptitude Tests (New York: John Wiley, 1966); and David C. McClelland, The Achieving Society (Princeton, N.J.: Van Nostrand, 1961).

5. David C. McClelland, "Business Drive and National Achievement," HBR July-August 1962, p. 99.

6. Harry R. Tosdal, "How to Design the Salesman's Compensation Plan," HBR September-October 1953, p. 61.

7. "Sales Compensation" (Mount Kisco, N.Y.: Research Institute of America, 1975).

8. John P. Steinbrink, "How to Pay Your Sales Force," HBR July-August 1978, p. 111; and Richard C. Smyth, "Financial Incentives for Salesmen," HBR January-February 1968, p. 109.

9. Tosdal, "Salesman's Compensation Plan," HBR.

Compensation plan design

In 1953, Harry Tosdal wrote that "a large portion of sales managers seem dissatisfied with their present compensation plans . . . unfortunately, there is no nice or easy solution." [6] The problem of designing effective sales compensation programs has not been solved since Tosdal's observation 27 years ago. A recent Research Institute of America (RIA) study indicates that 24% of all responding companies had redesigned their sales pay plans during the past 2 years—the same percentage of change as had been reported in its 1971 survey.[7] The 1975 RIA study comments that "companies do considerable milling about and searching for the combination that will give them the best results."

Designing an effective sales compensation program, however, is a complex management assignment. All the sales executives we talked to expressed concern about whether plans would increase immediate sales and, if so, whether they would sacrifice the development of long-term accounts. Other areas of concern were equitable pay, how a plan should be communicated, and what percent of total take-home pay should be a fixed base. They also worried about whether incentive plans would interfere with the introduction of new product lines and strategy changes and, finally, whether money or status is the real motivator.

We couldn't attempt to answer all these pragmatic and challenging questions and focused only on identifying whether incentive compensation would be a more effective motivator for salespeople than straight salary. Straight salary is a fixed, agreed-on amount of gross pay that does not vary from week to week during a definite period of time. With an incentive compensation plan all or a certain percentage of a salesperson's income varies in relation to that individual's performance.

Much has been written about the design of sales pay programs.[8] According to Tosdal, the two most widely used compensation designs—straight salary and commission—both offer definite advantages.[9] Straight salary provides security and reduces employees' worries about fluctuations in take-home pay. It is also simple in design and administration and avoids questions of parity in pay across different functions in the same company. On the other hand, commissions provide a powerful incentive. Studies conducted in 1953 by Tosdal and in 1975 by RIA

Exhibit III
Relation of effort to task clarity and personality*

	Hours spent in selling or in sales-related activities per week
A. Task clarity	
Clear – business products	58
Unclear – transportation services	42
B. Personality	
Higher need to achieve	53
Lower need to achieve	47

*See the ruled insert for an explanation of the variable used.

show that most managers favor some form of incentive compensation:

Type of Plan	Tosdal (1,254 companies)	RIA (9,000 companies)
Straight salary	20%	24%
Straight commission	24	20
Combination of both	56	56

Although sales managers make strikingly similar choices of plans, they continue to search for the "right" compensation plan just as they did in the early 1950s. A senior vice president of one company participating in our study comments:

"The board of directors asked me to develop a financial package for the managers of a recently acquired subsidiary. Our consultants showed us a number of complex incentive plans, but the basic question I have is whether the extra dollars invested in incentive pay will result in return on investment in terms of motivation. If not, we should forget about all the incentive pay plans and use straight salary. But the interesting question is on what basis do we decide to go straight salary or incentive."

Our findings demonstrate:

> In general, incentive pay is a more effective motivator than straight salary.

> The ability of incentive pay to act as a motivator is very much influenced by the nature of the selling task.

Exhibit IV shows that sales representatives in the business products and transportation services companies that paid on incentive had only slightly higher levels of motivation than sales representatives in the other two companies studied that paid on straight salary.

The true power of incentive pay surfaces when we take into account the nature of the sales task.

Exhibit IV
How design of compensation plan as well as incentive plan, combined with tasks of different clarity, relate to effort

	Hours spent selling or in sales-related activities per week
A. Plan	
Incentive compensation	51
Straight salary	48
B. Incentive plan and task	
Clear task (business products) with incentive compensation	62
Unclear task (transportation services) with incentive compensation	43

In the business products organization where the sales task is clear, incentive pay has a much larger motivational impact than the incentive program in the transportation services company where the sales task is unclear.

Sales representatives' comments support our analysis. A salesperson in the transportation company with the incentive plan states: "None of us, including the manager, believes in the commission. It's more of a game than a science. All of us like the extra dollars, but in terms of motivation, the bonus has little impact."

The comments of a salesperson paid on incentive in the business equipment industry are different: "There is no doubt in my mind that our company's incentive and recognition systems have a big influence on motivation. I used to earn about $15,000; this year I will hit $25,000 to $30,000. I feel proud about this, and I like being able to have a chance to make a good dollar. I am in control of my own destiny."

Compare this statement with the comments of another sales representative who is paid a straight salary in the other business equipment company: "Our management needs to rethink its philosophy of sales compensation. It really bothers me that I don't get paid for results. In my territory, sales are up 64% over last year. The sales manager says I am doing a good job, but it's not reflected in my take-home pay. Maybe it's one of the reasons that in this office the people don't make too many sales calls."

Two implications stem from these findings. First, the design and implementation of a sales incentive system is time consuming and costly. If the sales task is unclear, the ability of an incentive to motivate is significantly diminished, which suggests that a straight salary would be more practical and less problematic. Second, sales pay must not be seen as an isolated variable but as part of a system. In this system, on-the-job performance is influenced not only by the design of the pay plan but also by characteristics of the sales task and the personality of the salespeople.

How these factors in combination influence the ability of pay to serve as a source of motivation is shown in *Exhibit V*. Our overall findings and comparative rankings are shown in *Exhibit VI*.

Quality of management

In recruiting and training their sales representatives, managers spend a lot of money—a good deal of which is often wasted due to ineffective sales supervision. Furthermore, because the salesperson's role can be especially frustrating, the first-line sales supervisor's role has additional importance. But little is known about what constitutes effective supervision in a sales setting.[10] In fact, most contemporary articles on sales management merely describe current fads and trends.

Because of this lack, we aimed a segment of our study at identifying what sales supervisors can do to contribute to the good performance of their subordinates. We identified the following skills as contributing toward effective leadership. Although the list is tentative, we include it because of the importance of first-line supervision and the "systems" nature of our findings:

☐ *Goal setting*—Sets high but attainable performance standards for subordinates and other groups. Gives responsibility and challenging assignments.

☐ *Evaluation*—Provides timely and frequent feedback to subordinates on their progress toward established goals.

☐ *Coaching*—Assists the sales representative to identify training needs and areas for improvement, particularly in regard to personal selling skills and time management. Structures opportunities for the application of newly learned skills. Rewards improvements.

☐ *Empathize*—Shows personal concern and sensitivity to others. Develops constructive working relationships with subordinates. Knows when to withdraw and let the salespeople try it on their own.

☐ *Know-how*—Demonstrates a thorough knowledge of personal selling and marketing. Keeps abreast of events both inside and outside the organization that may affect the success of subordinates.

A sales management system

With our results in mind, we suggest managers adopt a multifunctional approach to achieve the greatest possible improvement in sales performance.[11] Managers need to stress the positive effects of task design, personality, and compensation—in that order. To design such a plan, managers should assess the current level of each variable, how much each variable would have to be modified to bring it up to the maximum realizable goals, and the costs associated with that degree of modification of each factor.

John Roche, manager of marketing training and development at Emery Air Freight, applied such a framework in 1976. Before then each Emery salesperson was assigned a territory with hundreds of accounts. The process of selecting accounts for sales calls was understandably vague and difficult. As a result, many calls resulted in dead ends with a comparable high ratio of failure to success.

The clouds hanging over the sales representatives' success were compounded by two problems with measurement:

1. Because it took from three to five months for feedback on sales to reach them, salespeople—who need to know how they are doing from day to day—could not get a psychologically meaningful picture of their performance.

2. Even when they did, it was often impossible to determine whether they or the salespeople on the other end should get credit for the sale.

A senior vice president and general manager of Emery described it this way: "Every day we move thousands of shipments to customers all over the world. We don't really know which sales representative closed the sale. For example, a city like New York . . . there are hundreds of shipments in and out of there every day which the New York sales force may have had nothing to do with. Perhaps it was our sales rep or a truck driver in Kansas City who is generating business into New York. We have come to the conclusion that we cannot equitably measure a salesperson in terms of revenue or shipment counts because no one really knows who is responsible for

10. Walker, Gilbert, and Ford, "Motivation and Performance in Industrial Selling," p. 157.

11. Gene W. Dalton and Paul R. Lawrence, *Motivation and Control in Organizations* (Homewood, Ill.: Richard D. Irwin, 1971), p. 291.

Exhibit V
How incentive plan, in combination with personality and task clarity, affects effort

Motivating factor	Hours spent selling or in sales-related activities per week
Straight salary (two companies)	48
Incentive (two companies)	51
Incentive plan + clear task	62
Incentive plan + clear task + high need to achieve	65

Exhibit VI
Overall findings for task clarity, personality, and compensation in relation to effort

Motivating factor	Hours spent selling or in sales-related activities per week
Task	
Clear	58
Unclear	42
Personality	
High need to achieve	53
Low need to achieve	47
Compensation	
Incentive	51
Straight salary	48

closing the sale on 50% of the shipments that move across our docks."

The high risk of failure, large account load, and imprecise feedback considerably decreased the scope in which a salesperson could take effective individual action—the key feature of the selling task. On a scale of 1 to 10 (with 10 high and 1 low) salespeople rated their individual control over their sales results at just above 3.

In applying its systems approach, Emery management first authorized a redesign of the sales task in three offices and an evaluation of the impact on sales performance. The design included:

□ *Target accounts*—Salespeople were instructed to sell to a smaller group of customers. Each selected account, however, had a large potential for increased business.

□ *Feedback & measurement*—A computer-based information system was designed to provide timely updates to salespeople on their weekly performance in relation to their targets.

□ *Planning*—The salespeople were taught how to determine potential value from their accounts and how to plan their time and calls to maximize sales results.

This design improved the marketing capability of the sales force and also allowed the achievement-oriented salespeople to function at greater potential. In other words, the job was structured toward a higher probability that the salespeople would be able to measure and control their own success or failure.

The results of the job redesign in the three offices of Emery are impressive, in terms of both the salespeoples' sense of successful control over their task and their improved sales. The salespeoples' rating of their individual control over results climbed from an initial low of 3.2 to a consistent 8.9. In terms of shipments, the three offices moved to among the top producers in their respective regions, increasing shipments an average of 34.7% from 1978 to 1979 (see *Exhibit VII*).

The initial results and the sales force's acceptance of the job redesign led James J. Brown, senior vice president and general manager, to redesign the sales task throughout the company. Brown said that: "In addition to increasing the motivation and productivity of the sales force, we find a positive by-product is the availability to management of timely and accurate information. It helps us forecast, staff, respond to customers' needs and competitors' actions, and direct the sales force toward specific prospects in profitable, growing industries."

Success: a sum of the parts

Although we have identified four factors that both individually and in combination have a large impact on salesperson motivation, it is not clear *why* they work together the way they do. We believe, however, that task clarity, personality, compensation plan, and quality of management are important because of the relationships expressed in the following chart:

Salesperson effort expended ←
↓
Actual sales results
↓
Reported sales results
↓
Rewards and recognition ────┘

Exhibit VII
Percent increase in number of shipments in three Emery offices during the previous year*

Control offices	Test sites	Difference
6.24%	One 9.23%	47.9%
6.35	Two 8.41	32.4
6.35	Three 7.86	23.8
6.31 (increase)	8.50 (increase)	34.7 (average difference in sales increases)

*Shipments were used instead of revenues to control for inflation. Also there were no significant pricing or service changes in the test sites.

1. *Clear tasks* ensure that the linkage between the effort expended and the actual sales results is good and tight. Task clarity also makes it easier to measure and report sales results accurately and makes a good measurement system possible.

2. *Need for achievement* makes good salespeople. They thrive in a system in which the effort they expend clearly relates to results.

3. *Incentive compensation* makes a strong link between reward (and often recognition) and expended effort (through reported actual sales results).

4. *Good management* ensures accurate reporting of actual sales results, equitable rewards for reported sales results, and valuable recognition of these results.

Rewards and recognition motivate the salesperson to increase the effort expended. Willingness to do the work is only part of generating good sales results, however; salespeople must also be able to do the work. Thus good training, both in a center and in the field, is necessary to enable salespeople to accomplish their goals. Such a comprehensive sales system will generate a capable, motivated, and successful sales force—with rewards for both the individual salesperson and the company.▽

Make the sales task clear

Benson P. Shapiro and Stephen X. Doyle

Mr. Shapiro is professor of business administration and head of the required MBA marketing course at the Harvard Business School. Mr. Doyle is president of SXD Associates, a management consulting firm in Great Neck, New York. The study on which this article is based received financial support from the Associates of the Harvard Business School and the Western Electric Fund.

In an earlier HBR article we reported that sales task clarity has a greater impact on the motivation of field salespeople than ego drive or compensation method.[1] In addition, we reported that sales task clarity can reinforce the effects of good recruiting and selection because it can make recruits with high ego drive work harder and better. Furthermore, it can reinforce a performance-oriented compensation system. On the other hand, an imprecise task can prevent even the most clever sales compensation system from working well.

Some sales tasks by their nature are less distinct than others. A drug detailer who calls on a doctor to suggest that she prescribe a particular medicine, for example, receives delayed feedback. Without a later audit of prescriptions written by the doctor for that product and competing ones, it is hard to discover whether the sale was ever made. Another example of low task clarity comes from selling electricity-generating equipment. The sale takes months or years and involves many people.

In this sequel to the 1980 article we turn our attention to three important aspects of sales task clarity: its definition and measurement, its impact on motivation and performance, and ways to enhance it so as to improve sales force motivation and performance.

Definition & measurement

A task is clear if the relationship between a salesperson's effort and the reported results of that effort is not ambiguous. Clarity is a function of the impact of a person's efforts on sales results, of the timeliness of performance feedback, and of the accuracy of the feedback.

We designed a questionnaire to measure these three aspects and administered it to salespeople and their supervisors in four companies. Two of the sales forces sold business products, the other two sold transportation services. All the companies were profitable and were industry leaders with national reputations and respected products.

The business products salespeople received clear and accurate feedback weekly about their performance, which was relatively easy to measure (by dollar volume of orders booked). The transport services companies had no definite, objective measures because of the difficulty of correctly crediting the revenue from millions of (usually small) shipments to the various salespersons. It was hard to discover whether a sale was made through the shipper or the receiver of the merchandise. Moreover, the time between a sales call and a purchase of the service by telephone – not directly through the salesperson – varied considerably.

1 "What Counts Most in Motivating Your Sales Force," HBR May-June 1980, p. 133.

Motivation & performance

Motivation is difficult to define and hard to measure. Consequently, in trying to determine whether differences in sales task clarity are associated with differences in sales force motivation, we used multiple measures. They were sales performance against goal, supervisor's performance evaluation, amount of time worked per week, and strength of salesperson's belief that effort would be rewarded.

Salespeople in the two business products organizations scored 30% to 60% higher on the motivation measures than did their counterparts in the transportation companies. All four companies looked for recruits with a strong need to achieve and big ego drives, so the differences in motivation evidently came from differences in sales task clarity, not recruiting and selection practices.

(As our previous article explained at length, the type of pay plan – incentive versus straight salary – also had less impact than the clarity of the task. Task clarity was 50% more important in determining motivation than personality, and nearly three times as important as type of pay plan. We therefore are confident in saying that clarity of task is the most important element in salesperson motivation.)

When the elements of the job were indistinct, the salespeople did not know where they stood and could not get reinforcement from news of their performance. A sales representative of one of the transportation services companies said, "Selling in this industry is like living in a dream. Getting ahead is a matter of luck and politics. It's discouraging."

In the business products companies, the sales reps remained an average of 3.3 years, versus 1.1 in the transport services organizations. A district sales manager of one of the latter commented, "Turnover is a real problem. We hire aggressive young trainees and fire them up with training. When they get out on the street, however, frustration becomes a problem. These people want to know how they are doing and how competitive they are. Many of the reps who quit are uncomfortable with our type of selling."

Ways to enhance it

Judging from our research, there are four areas where management can make tasks clear.

1 **Deployment.** Often salespeople are assigned territories with only geographic boundaries and are given little more than "hunting licenses" within those boundaries. We suggest that important parts of task clarity are a limitation on the number of accounts for which each person has responsibility and specification of goals for each of these target accounts.

Few sales representatives can regularly handle more than about 50 accounts in a situation in which a real sales effort, instead of a cursory presentation effort, is necessary. Yet some companies assign several hundred accounts to each salesperson or give them "all" the accounts in a geographic area. Doing so can only lead to frustration as the salespeople realize they have no set priorities and are powerless to control their performance.

The more specific the account coverage, the better. It is important, for example, to list the accounts for each rep. If necessary, a part of the defined task can be the salesperson's responsibility to add to the list some number, perhaps five, of qualified prospects. The important thing is that the salespeople understand which accounts they are responsible for and will be judged by.

2 **Account management.** The salespeople must be charged with clear goals to accomplish at each account—total sales goals, activity goals, sales goals by product, and so on. As we have seen, the more measurable the goals, the clearer the task definition and the greater the motivation. Goals can, of course, go beyond sales to include matters such as presentations, placement of promotions, and penetration to specified members of the buying organization.

Another criterion, attainability, deserves note. It is dysfunctional to include in a person's goals tasks over which he or she has little or no control. Frustration and anxiety are the result. If, for example, salespeople are judged by shipments to accounts (not by orders or bookings) and the shipping schedule varies with the production control organization's ability or inclination, the salespeople will be disgruntled because the task is unclear.

3 **Information system.** The information system furnishes the connection between actual performance and reported performance. A poor information system will destroy the salesperson's perception of an unblocked linkage between effort and results.

The information system, more than any other tool, determines the timeliness and accuracy of feedback, which are vital to task clarity. An element of randomness added by the system to the quality of the performance reports ruins the accuracy of the feedback. Delay in the information flow reduces the salespeople's ability to remember their effort (at both an intellectual and an emotional level) and to relate it to the reported results.

4 **Field sales management.** To ensure task clarity for each salesperson, the field sales manager can use a variety of management mechanisms and processes. Most of these center on the goal-setting, feedback, coaching, and appraisal cycle. They include management by objectives, performance appraisal, and monthly reviews.

Of course, they require a commitment by the field sales managers, which begins with deployment and account planning. The manager tailors the task to the particular salesperson, sales territory, and accounts. Perhaps even more important from a motivational point of view, the manager ensures through a dialogue with the salesperson that he or she understands and accepts the task as laid out. In the case of goods like the aforementioned generating equipment, the challenge of clarifying the sales task will test the cleverness and ingenuity of any sales manager.

At the other end of the cycle—appraisal—the manager helps the salesperson to interpret the results and relate them to the defined task and the salesperson's effort. So, the sales manager helps to clarify and amplify the definition of the task and the measurement of results.

Naturally, an organization's sales managers must understand *their* task and be trained to accomplish it. But no sales manager, regardless of ability or training, can work effectively with a poor information system or a compensation system that rewards people haphazardly instead of for clearly defined results.

Sales task clarity is generally controllable by management. Moreover, it may be one of the most powerful motivational tools available to policy-level sales and marketing executives. ▽

Motivating
Manufacturing
Employees

Kratylus automates his urnworks

Thereby throwing Nikias out of work and sparking a Socratic dialogue on productivity and productiveness

Tolly Kizilos

Little did Kratylus know, when he contracted in Corinth to buy some foot-operated potter's wheels for his workshop, that his capital investment would become the subject of a spirited discussion among four Athenians touching on such topics as olive harvesting, burial mound building, input-output measurement, and participative management. Formerly, 20 workers in Kratylus's operation turned out 200 urns a day; now, with the new pulley-equipped devices, 12 employees can do the job.

What is productivity? How can you measure an individual's contribution toward a goal? How can an employer further human productiveness? These are the difficult questions that arise from the sacking of Nikias and seven others. Besides him, those airing the issues are Ipponikos, a rich landowner; Kallias, a politician and member of the Assembly; and Socrates, the philosopher.

Mr. Kizilos is the director of organizational development at the Systems and Research Center of Aerospace and Defense, Honeywell, Inc. A Honeywell employee for 24 years, he has held various positions, including manager of human resource development and ombudsman of the Systems and Research Center. Kizilos also serves on the corporate board for organizational development. In his work he focuses on organizational change through the implementation of participative management.

Illustrations by Edward Gorey.

Kallias: Here comes Nikias, troubled as usual about some social injustice or other.

Socrates: Good morning, Nikias. Isn't it a bit early in the day to be looking so troubled?

Nikias: Good morning, my friends, if you can call good a morning on which you lose your job.

Ipponikos: Sit down, Nikias, and tell us what happened. Remember what Socrates always says: "Nothing bad in this world is uncontaminated by good."

Nikias: I know what Socrates says, but it doesn't make sense to me just now. I don't know what will happen. I showed up for work at Kratylus's urnworks this morning, as I've done for three years, and he told me and seven others that we were no longer needed. He's installed some new foot-operated potter's wheels with pulleys, so he doesn't need as many people to do the work. Just like that, I'm unemployed.

Kallias: It wasn't all that sudden, though, was it, Nikias? I heard Kratylus almost a month ago talking openly at the agora about the new wheels he was buying from Corinth. It was no secret that he was going to install them to raise productivity. He had to do it, he told me, or he'd go out of business. I realize that you and a few others will suffer for a while, but he has to increase the productivity of his business or everyone working for him could end up without a job. And if he and others don't become more productive, Athens itself will take a backseat to Corinth and other cities, and all its citizens will suffer the consequences.

Nikias: We knew about it, all right, but we were hoping there would be other jobs we could do. Is it more productive to have people out of work, doing nothing, than to have them gainfully employed? How can the city's productivity grow if a lot of people are out of work? As far as I'm concerned, that kind of narrow-minded productivity increase helps no one but Kratylus; it just feeds his greed.

Kallias: Come now, Nikias; you can't possibly mean that! Productivity gains, no matter where, benefit everyone in the long run. You'll find another job soon, or Kratylus's business will expand and he'll need more workers to operate the faster wheels.

Socrates: Is productivity then both good and evil? Is it both the requirement for the workers' prosperity and the cause of their misfortunes?

Ipponikos: Ah, Socrates, how cleverly you always pose your questions—so pregnant with answers of your choosing! Why don't you go on and say that this is impossible, therefore productivity is either good or evil and, consequently, only one of our friends here can be right?

Socrates: Because, my dear Ipponikos, there is always a chance that a pregnant question will deliver a revealing answer. I find that I always discover new things as I grow older.

Kallias: Well, I'm always suspicious about ambiguous concepts. Productivity is either good or evil, and only one of us is right. Otherwise the concept is meaningless.

Ipponikos: People can always stretch the meaning of words enough to understand and agree with each other. All it takes is a common culture and goodwill.

Kallias: You aren't so bad at clever arguments yourself, Ipponikos. You imply that if we can't understand and agree with each other, it doesn't mean that some of us are wrong but that some are barbarians or rascals, or both. But perhaps you didn't mean that?

Nikias: If this is going to be a battle of wits, count me out.

Socrates: Nikias is right. Let's abandon generalities, which make philosophy irrelevant, and search for the meaning of productivity. Perhaps productivity is such an elusive concept that we can reach only a partial understanding of it, which, however, is acceptable to all of us. Let us be hopeful.

Ipponikos: With an ideologue like Kallias in the discussion, I'm afraid it'll be a waste of time.

Nikias: So is what we're doing right now. Let's discuss the issue instead of arguing over trivia.

Μισθοί καί προϊόντα

Kallias: I'll tell you what productivity is, Socrates, or at least what it means to me—take it as you like. It's not such a difficult concept. It's simply the ratio of useful work output for a given valuable input. The higher the output for the same input, the higher the productivity is.

Take, for example, Kratylus's urnworks. I know something about his business because occasionally he asks for my opinion. Kratylus produces about 200 urns a day and used to employ about 20 workers. If he can produce the same number of urns with half the work force, then he doubles his shop's productivity. It's as simple as that.

Ipponikos: It's so simple, it's idiotic. Whose productivity has he increased? Nikias isn't productive anymore. He worked hard and still got laid off. Kratylus's productivity gain is Nikias's productivity loss.

Nikias: More productivity for Kratylus means more satisfaction of his greed.

Kallias: I don't understand what's happening to us. If we are here to denigrate Kratylus, I want no part of it.

Socrates: The path to the truth is often obscured by thorny bushes, Kallias.

Kallias: I know it's hard to be objective right now, but the facts are irrefutable. When you were working for Kratylus—I'm sure very hard—you weren't very productive because you were using a slow wheel to shape the urns. You were paid wages to produce something that cost so much it couldn't be sold easily. Activity isn't productivity, Nikias.

What's needed is more output for a given input; what's needed is more drachmas from the sale of urns per drachma of wages. Now you produce nothing, but your wages are also nothing; so, it makes no sense to talk about your productivity. Only when you get paid to produce something of value, that is, when there's an input and an output, can we talk meaningfully about productivity.

Ipponikos: This input-output stuff may be useful when talking about machines or oxen, but it makes no sense when we're discussing human beings. Productivity means productive activity. Human beings can be very productive even when they're supported by handouts. Why, only two weeks ago I heard that the geometer Diomedes, a pauper, mind you, if there ever was one, invented an instrument for measuring angles he calls a theodolite. I heard Telemachus say it will save thousands of workdays for his surveying crew when they're setting the boundaries of farmers' fields all around Attica. Diomedes received no wages—no input, as you would say, Kallias—but does that mean we can't talk about his productivity? He *is* productive, very productive.

Kallias: Of course he is, my dear Ipponikos. Your example of Diomedes is precisely what I've been looking for to make my point. Maximum output with minimum possible input yields the highest productivity.

Nikias: So, productivity according to you is using up people. Humanity subordinated to the goddess of productivity. Perhaps you'd like to add another goddess to the 12 Olympians? It wouldn't surprise me.

Kallias: I said minimum *possible* input, not minimum input. Possible is the essential....

Ipponikos: I don't understand why you keep using inputs and outputs when you talk about human beings, Kallias. We could never define such things for humans, capable of an infinite variety and an infinite number of possible inputs and outputs, none of them exactly predictable. No man can be bound by defining him in terms of input and output. "Man is the measure of all things," as Protagoras said—he cannot himself be measured.

Nikias: But to Kratylus and others who own shops, Ipponikos, there's little difference among men, beasts, or machines. A person at work is told exactly what input he'll have (that is, what wages he'll be paid), exactly what he has to do, and what he's expected to produce. That's what happens when you work for someone else; you're dehumanized.

Kallias: You're too angry to contribute to this discussion, Nikias.

Ipponikos: Since when has anger been proven to be an obstacle in the search for truth?

Socrates: Nikias agrees with you, Ipponikos, that man is fundamentally different from the machine, and one of the reasons is that only machines have finite and measurable inputs and outputs by design.

Ipponikos: It's even more fundamental than that: Kallias talks about wages as inputs, but that's so narrow-minded it's absurd. People can get more than wages for doing their jobs; they can get satisfaction, learning, enjoyment; they can be frightened or encouraged by what happens around them; they can be made to feel stronger or weaker by the actions of others. Their productive activity is often the result of all these impressions, shaped by thinking, feeling, and judgment. And as for their output, sometimes it's so unpredictable as to instill awe, admiration, and delight.

Kallias: I'm really surprised by your views, Ipponikos. It seems that Protagoras and the other sophists have clouded your thoughts.

Ipponikos: I can do without your sarcasm, Kallias. Do me the courtesy of treating me like a person who can think for himself. If you have something to say about my views, say it without insinuations.

Kallias: I will, my friend, I most certainly will. You are espousing a very irresponsible view and I couldn't possibly avoid commenting on it. According to you, a workshop owner should hire workers and pay them wages, but demand nothing specific of them. Some of them may want to loaf; others may decide to take up playwriting or singing instead of making urns; and some of them may even choose to work and produce urns once in a while. Now and then, perhaps, a worker will invent a new tool that improves the quality of urns or the productivity of the shop, but there will be no guarantees. And the wages have to keep coming steadily, guaranteed.

Is this a responsible way to run a business? Could the workshop owner entrust his future to the whims of his workers? The workers have no stake in the business and, if the shop went broke, they could leave at a moment's notice to take jobs elsewhere. And what about those who really work hard to produce urns and urns alone? Wouldn't this irresponsible approach be unfair to them?

Ipponikos: You talk as if the workers want to loaf and behave irresponsibly toward the owner and their fellow workers. You don't trust them.

Kallias: Not everyone is responsible and trustworthy.

Ipponikos: Perhaps not. But if the owner trusts his people and rewards them fairly, I believe that the workers would strive to do their best for the business. Some will be less productive than others, but the productivity of the whole place will be higher when people feel free to use all their talents and skills. As for fairness, the workers themselves will set standards and require that everyone pull his weight.

Socrates: I hear a lot of views being expressed, but no conclusions. If this were a workshop, its productivity would be very low, and some of us, I fear, would have to be replaced by more productive philosophers,

probably from Sparta. Can't we first agree on what productivity means?

Kallias: It's apparent to me, Socrates, that this isn't possible with Ipponikos and Nikias present. If you and I were alone, we could be more productive than the whole city of Sparta discussing the issue.

Socrates: You and I, Kallias, might come up with conclusions very fast, but the quality of our conclusions might not be as high as it can be with our friends here contributing their ideas.

Kallias: Sooner or later, I suppose, we'll have to talk about effectiveness and efficiency. I believe that productivity is high only when both efficiency and effectiveness are high.

Socrates: All right, let's see what you mean. Suppose you hire me for a drachma a day to pick olives fallen from your olive trees in Eleusis. While I'm working, I notice that the fence protecting your property from the wild pigs is down. Pigs can get into your fields and devour the ripe olives that have fallen on the ground. Because I think this is more urgent and because I'm much better at repairing fences than gathering olives, I decide to fix your fence instead.

I work hard all day long and by sunset I'm done and I'm sitting on a rock admiring the good work I did. You return from your day's debates at the Assembly and find me in this contemplative pose. You see that I have picked no olives but have fixed your fence. The question is, will you pay me as we agreed or not?

Kallias: Of course not. You changed our contract arbitrarily. I could suffer losses because of that. You shouldn't have changed the output.

Nikias: He means he didn't want you to think; do only what you were told. Be a machine or a mindless ox.

Socrates: But a contract is a contract, Nikias. What if he was counting on me to pick the olives so he could deliver them to someone who had a contract with him to buy them that same evening? I was productive, all right, but not productive doing what we agreed on. In that, my productivity was zero. So isn't it true that productivity has meaning only when there's an agreement on the inputs or wages, and the outputs or the goals?

Kallias: Of course it is.

Ipponikos: And if someone produces something very valuable without any agreement?

Socrates: It appears that it doesn't make sense to talk about productivity when there's no agreement, explicit or implicit.

Kallias: Exactly. Productivity pertains to work toward a goal. There must be expectation of output and fulfillment of that expectation.

Ὁ παραμυθάς δοῦλος

Socrates: I'm glad you agree with what I said. But I have some difficulty with it, and you may be able to help me. It has to do with something that happened when they were building the mound commemorating the glorious dead who fell at the battle of Marathon.

Kallias: I can't for the life of me imagine what Marathon has to do with productivity. Are you serious?

Ipponikos: Perhaps you've hit on your problem, Kallias—lack of imagination.

Socrates: Please, allow me to continue. Everything is related to everything else, say some philosophers, and I'll be happy to explain what I mean if you let me.

Nikias: You are the last person on earth I would want to stop, Socrates. You're usually able to deliver what you promise, but even if you weren't, you're too stubborn to be stopped.

Socrates: I'll take that as praise, Nikias, and go on. After Pericles gave his marvelous funeral oration on that hallowed ground, he left behind General Meno from Orchomenos in charge of 100 slaves and ordered him to build the mound in 30 days. Meno was determined to obey the order even though he estimated that the project would take twice that time. It is said that General Meno became a tyrant with the slaves, driving them ruthlessly to work.

One day, during an inspection of the project, he discovered a slave who sat on the nearby edge of the marsh in blissful repose. Furious, he ordered his lieutenants to flog him until he was hardly alive. General Meno wanted to make this laggard an example for the other slaves, demonstrating to them that because the slave didn't produce, he made everyone else work harder. "He is a weight upon the earth!" he shouted for all to hear, using Homer's words.

Kallias: I still don't see....

Socrates: Then one of the most productive slaves stepped forward and asked to speak. General Meno could hardly hold back his anger, but because he valued this slave greatly he allowed him to say his piece. "This man, sir," the slave said, pointing to his doomed comrade, "is one of the most productive slaves you have. It is true that he neither sweats nor strains his back digging and shoveling earth, but he contributes to the building of the mound more than anyone else."

"And how does he do this? Gazing at his belly button while you and the others break your backs?" the general demanded.

"You see, General," the slave said with conviction, "he is a storyteller, not a digger. If he was shoveling dirt with all his might, he couldn't do in a day more than I do in an hour. But after work, when we all return to camp, dog-tired, miserable, and hopeless—for what can we expect from the future but more bondage and more misery?—when we are gathered around the campfire at night, this man spins tales of hope for us and makes our lot bearable. We listen to him and dream of a better life after we end this project. He makes our burdens lighter, and we can fall asleep with dreams of freedom in our heads. Next day we are ready for work, believing that if our work pleases you and the Athenians, we may some day gain our freedom."

Kallias: I think I'm beginning....

Socrates: Please let me finish. "So," the slave went on, "this man does his part. If you beat him senseless, or cripple him, or—worst of fates!—kill him, who will keep us hoping, dreaming, and working? If hope vanishes, punishment and death hold no fear, General. We may not be able to build your mound. Think of that, sir, and allow this man to go on producing what he is best able to produce: tales of hope. You need him as much as, if not more than, we do."

So spoke the valued slave, and General Meno listened. He ordered his lieutenants to release the man, who went on to tell tales until the project was finished—exactly on time. The question, dear Kallias, is this: Was the storytelling slave productive or not?

Kallias: Of course he was productive, probably the most productive of all. He contributed to the achievement of the goal, didn't he? Whether he knew it or not, he worked toward the same goal as all the other slaves.

Ὁρισμός τοῦ σκοποῦ

Socrates: So, you say, productivity is work toward a goal. You wouldn't pay me for fixing your fence because you had set the goal as gathering fallen olives. What about here? Here, the goal was to build a mound, just as Kratylus's goal is to produce urns, and ours is to come up with the truth. But this slave wasn't building the mound, I wasn't gathering olives, and some workers at Kratylus's urnworks may not be producing as many urns as their fellows.

Yet you just told us that this slave was probably the most productive slave working on the mound. Could I have been more productive to you by fixing your fence? Could Nikias, who wasn't producing as much with his old wheel, and I, bumbling now on my way to the truth, be more productive than others who achieve stated goals? Could it be, Kallias, that Nikias, now that he is searching for the truth with us, is more productive to our city (and of course to Kratylus) than when he was making urns?

Kallias: I thought you would twist things sooner or later, Socrates, and I've been alert to it.

Ipponikos: It won't help you much, Kallias. You're too efficient to be effective. If you're sure you know the truth and you're sitting here searching for it, you are obviously wasting your time, and your productivity has to be nil.

Kallias: Leave your sophistry for later, Ipponikos, and let me respond to Socrates. It seems to me, Socrates, that you are mixing two kinds of productivity. Yes, Nikias is more productive to our city when he's searching for the truth with us than he would be if he were doing nothing. To the extent that Kratylus is a citizen of Athens, he benefits from Nikias's philosophizing as does every other citizen. But Nikias is not productive to Kratylus because he simply isn't making urns any more.

Socrates: But if our city is more productive, doesn't Kratylus have a better chance to sell his wares? And if that is so, isn't it fair to say that Kratylus, as the owner of the workshop, is benefiting from Nikias's philosophizing?

Kallias: Productivity loses all meaning if you put it that way. Humanity benefits from anything productive anyone does. But I still say that productivity is a useful concept only when it's limited to specific goals achieved by specific persons.

Ipponikos: Come on, Kallias, use your imagination! Think of all the ways the workers, even at Kratylus's workshop, can contribute to the production and sale of urns even when they're not actually making or selling urns. No one can say whether a person is productive by just looking at him or by measuring only specific inputs and outputs.

Kallias: Use your reason, Ipponikos.

Socrates: But Kallias, how can you tell when a person is doing something or nothing? And how can you say that a person can be productive to the city but not to Kratylus's workshop, which is, after all, a part of the city? And how can you tell if a person is productive when the goals set for that person are different from the goals toward which a person works? One can still contribute to the goals if one interprets goals more broadly.

Kallias: All I know is that somehow or other using a new wheel makes Kratylus's workshop more productive because he can lay off Nikias and some other workers and still produce the same number of urns. Then Nikias, as Kratylus had thought, finds something else to do—philosophize, in this case—and he becomes productive again to the city and to Kratylus, because he is also a citizen.

Socrates: That's well put, Kallias. But if Nikias is now productive to the city, he must be paid for his productivity. Yet I haven't heard of anyone willing to put philosophers on the public payroll. Would you propose that the Assembly pass a law to do that? It certainly would help us all, Nikias and me in particular, since we are not influential politicians like you or wealthy landowners like Ipponikos.

Ipponikos: It's not only philosophers who are productive and should be compensated but also geometers, poets, musicians, and all kinds of other people who work with their minds.

Kallias: Everyone would become a freeloader.

Nikias: Are you saying that all thinkers are freeloaders?

Kallias: Don't be absurd, Nikias. I'm saying that people with no talent for geometry or music or bent for philosophical search would claim to be geometers, musicians, and philosophers in order to collect money from the city and avoid sweating in workshops and fields. Since there is no way to measure their output, no one could tell whether Socrates was more productive than the man who sweeps the steps leading up to the Parthenon. The sweeper could claim, for example, that gazing at the blue sky was helpful in proving the Pythagorean theorem in a new way.

Socrates: And so we have arrived at a point where we must make distinctions: there is productivity and there is productivity, and unless we sort these out we will never come to any conclusions. There is productivity of persons who perform manual work with a physical output; productivity of persons whose output is thoughts, poems, songs, inventions, proofs, and so on; and productivity of groups, such as ours, organizations or institutions, such as Kratylus's workshop or our beloved city of Athens. These are the entities to which we have attached potential for productivity.

Nikias: I'll start by defining the productivity of manual workers.

Kallias: Their productivity depends simply on their output, be it urns made, olives picked, marble slabs quarried, or what have you, divided by the cost of production, which is mostly wages.

Nikias: You may think it's that simple, but I don't. Even a manual worker has a mind that he can use when he does his work. His productivity can be defined your way only if you rob him of his mind. If one does that by rigidly defining the input and the output, that is, if one dehumanizes him, then one can define his productivity accurately—so many urns per drachma of wages, so much earth moved to build a mound per loaf of bread, so many olives gathered per day's wage.

One can go even further and define the productivity of those workers who work with their intellect that way—so many plays written, or songs composed, or theorems proved, or philosophical conclusions reached per drachma. But remember, the only way this can be done is if you set rigid, unalterable inputs and outputs. If a philosopher wrote a poem and an urnmaker proved a theorem of geometry, their productivity would be nothing.

Ipponikos: In other words, Kallias, you have to choose between having a precise definition of productivity and missing a lot of good work, or having at best a sloppy definition and allowing other, unanticipated but valuable work to be encouraged.

Kallias: I can't believe this! You argue with the same cunning as some unscrupulous colleagues of mine in the Assembly. I will give you a precise definition that at the same time encourages all valuable work to proceed: set outputs that are to be met unless more valuable outputs are produced. General Meno set goals, but when a slave produced stories that helped the goal indirectly, the general recognized that his out-

put was more valuable than his manual output would have been in furthering the goal directly.

This way the worker whose output is supposed to be the production of urns will be rewarded when he produces urns or something else, a new potter's wheel or a great poem perhaps, which the person who set the goals and must pay for their accomplishment finds equally valuable or even more valuable than the production of urns. This is my position, and I challenge you to find fault with it!

Ἐπίτευξη τοῦ σκοποῦ

Socrates: It is indeed an excellent position, Kallias. You have said that productivity for an individual worker is his valuable output per given input. It is a good definition, but you haven't told us how the value of the output is determined or whether the person who evaluated it is competent to do so.

Ipponikos: I would hate to have Kratylus decide the relative value of ten urns versus Sophocles' *Antigone.*

Kallias: Again, your way of arguing is to ridicule. I'm getting annoyed with you, Ipponikos, and unless you change your ways I will have to bid you farewell and seek a more congenial discussion elsewhere.

Ipponikos: I apologize for my sarcasm, Kallias. But please, do respond to Socrates.

Kallias: I don't believe that shop owners are any less competent to evaluate the relative worth of urns and plays than anyone else. Judgment, after all, is one of the most important attributes one must have to succeed in business.

Socrates: Wouldn't it perhaps be better if the employer and the wage earner could discuss the value of the work or the productivity of the wage earner and agree on it? After all, the person who produces something may be the only one who can explain the purpose for which he produced that thing and judge its value from his perspective.

Kallias: That process might work in Socrates' ideal state, but I don't think it has a chance in Athens. The wage earner can discuss all you like him to discuss, but when the time comes to decide how productive he is, when it comes to making a decision on how much he should be paid, the one who has the power, who pays the wages, will have the final word.

Ipponikos: You say that those who have the power set the standards and you accuse *me* of arguing like the sophists? Why, what you just said is exactly what Thrasymachus teaches.

Kallias: Then I have to admit that even a sophist can be right, once.

Nikias: I've had enough of the sophists. I want to hear Socrates on what workers have to say about the value of their work.

Socrates: Even if we assume that power is what one needs to set standards, what I said still stands. The wage earner also has power because the employer needs him to be as productive as possible, not be a mere machine executing set goals. If the employer doesn't evaluate him correctly, the wage earner will cease coming up with new products, new methods, or new ideas, and the productivity of the organization will suffer. Since the employer cannot *make* the wage earner be creative or take the initiative, or modify goals to suit changed situations, he must ensure that the wage earner stays motivated. And the best way for the employer to achieve that is not to be arbitrary or authoritarian but to share his power of evaluation with him.

I see you're shaking your head, Kallias. When you reflect on these thoughts you may become less skeptical. In any case, it is an alternative way of settling the issue we were discussing. Productivity increases come not only from getting faster wheels in the workshops but also from workers such as Nikias who feel in a way like owners of the workshop. Isn't it then correct to say that productivity is defined by whatever reasonable input and output both wage earner and employer agree on?

Kallias: Though I don't believe that this process will work, I agree that it is worth an experiment to find out. But I don't think we have really defined productivity.

Nikias: If we have arrived at a conclusion....

Socrates: Definitions can get us only so far. It's the dialogue between well-meaning people that gains our ends. This is the process, it seems to me, that will also determine the productivity of organizations such as Kratylus's workshop or our beloved city of Athens. Plato may not agree entirely with me on this, but I believe that the productivity of Athens is great because we all partake in making the decisions that govern our lives. Democracy is a form of participation, and it's surprising that it hasn't been applied to our workshops in some appropriate form.

Kallias: Well, I have always felt that productivity was of great concern to both politics and business. If we set goals and compile a list of all the services our city provides for its citizens, then measure them....

Socrates: I doubt that it would be either possible or meaningful, Kallias. The evaluation of our city's productivity is in the hands of future generations. Whether we sink to oblivion or history remembers us is not predictable or determined by a list of services or the Assembly's definition of goals. Athens and other cities and states will live on if they encourage their citizens to excel in what they do best.

Nikias: Before you go any further with an encomium to our city, Socrates, I would like to know if anyone here intends to inform Kratylus of my contributions to our discourse and ask him whether he would reconsider his decision to lay me off. If this isn't anyone's intention, I'd like to move on and look for another job before my family has to beg for food.

Kallias: I can certainly talk to him about it. But would you be willing to moderate your demands on wages? At least until his workshop begins to make profits again?

Nikias: I'll do anything reasonable to keep my job, of course. But if the job could be a little more satisfying than what I used to do, or if I have some say on what I do and how I am evaluated, then I'll bear the load more comfortably and I may even turn out more urns than ever before.

Socrates: I'm sure, Nikias, that you're speaking the truth.

Kallias: Can anyone venture a guess as to our productivity in this discussion?

Socrates: We've done our best, and I believe we've reached some agreements. If we didn't answer all the questions and didn't solve all the problems, it isn't because we were unproductive but because some problems are beyond our reach. Sisyphus, who rolls his stone up the mountain only to have it roll back down, is not unproductive; he works as hard as he possibly can, doing everything a human being can do. If he isn't as productive as he could be, it's because the gods have chosen it to be that way. So with us; we have done as well as we can. The gods may allow others in the future to do better.

Nikias: If one could only eat the truth he produces....

Ipponikos: Of course one can, Nikias. All one has to do is make the truth wanted by many.

Kallias: Next time I'll ask Kratylus to join us. We should have more businessmen-philosophers around.

Socrates: It would be a wonderful thing to do. I pray for your success. ▽

Greater employee responsibility does not mean greater discretion over time and work.

The Human Costs of Manufacturing Reform

by Janice A. Klein

If there is anything more powerful than an idea whose time has come, it is one that is the product of wishful thinking. Ask any manager or management consultant what the related essentials of manufacturing reform are, and the answer will likely come back: a just-in-time approach to eliminating waste, rigorous statistical process control to improve quality, and increased employee participation and self-management. One manager I know was emphatic: "JIT, SPC, and worker involvement in production management are like the three legs of a milking stool. Each is critical. If any one of the three breaks or is missing, the others will fall down."

He was an operations manager, eager to tap his workers' knowledge. He also anticipated their enthusiasm. It seemed obvious to him that increased participation was precisely what workers wanted or would quickly come to want. Implicit in that view is the belief that reformed manufacturing is more

consistent with the moral ideal of "autonomy" than traditional manufacturing is.

Is it? That depends on what one means, precisely, by "participation": employee involvement, self-management, and teams. In the United States and Europe, most designers of employee participation programs think of teams as a way of *empowering* the work force. Companies involve workers in manufacturing reform by allowing team members a good deal of autonomy in managing daily activities—in scheduling the work and determining the procedures to carry it out.

In Japan, in contrast, where JIT and SPC have been used most extensively, employees are routinely organized into teams, but their involvement in workplace reform is typically restricted to suggestions for process improvement through structured quality control circles or *kaizen* groups. Individual Japanese workers have unprecedented responsibility. Yet it is hard to think of them

exercising genuine autonomy, that is, in the sense of independent self-management.

To be sure, managers can—and must—involve workers in workplace decisions. But the attack on waste, it must be understood, inevitably means more and more strictures on a worker's time and action. Our conventional Western notions of worker self-management on the factory floor are often sadly incompatible with them.

The engine plant

Nothing brought this point home to me more graphically than the case of an engine plant I've studied. Over ten years ago, a large engine company designed a greenfield site; high among its priorities were worker morale and participation. The organizational design included self-managing work teams, many provisions for multiskilled workers, a reasonably flat—not hierarchical—management structure, and an explicit commitment to a "factory culture" based on growth, trust, equity, and excellence. Workers met schedules they themselves helped to set, laid out their work space to suit themselves, and performed assembly tasks in the manner they thought best. Meanwhile, inventory buffers provided time for workers to participate in management decisions. The plant soon became a model for the corporation, outperforming its traditional manufacturing operations not only in improved quality and safety but also in reduced overhead.

In the early days, the plant was not under severe cost or delivery pressures; the primary focus was on producing a top-quality product in an enriching work environment. But with the oil embargo, a recession in the automobile industry, and intensified foreign competition, the corporation found it necessary to reduce its manufacturing costs drastically.

Janice A. Klein is an assistant professor at the Harvard Business School. Her last contribution to HBR (with Pamela A. Posey) was "Good Supervisors Are Good Supervisors—Anywhere" (November-December 1986).

Top management believed that JIT and SPC would improve the company's competitiveness and quality and decided to introduce these approaches throughout the corporation's facilities.

The plant workers, who were by now accustomed to taking the initiative, quickly responded by forming a number of groups to plan the implementation process. One group began by scanning literature, attending seminars, and visiting other companies that had implemented JIT and SPC. A second focused on the plant's work flow, taking on the challenge of improving fixtures and tooling to reduce setups on individual work stations. (It videotaped the operations of all the teams, whose members then viewed the tapes and brainstormed to find ways of reducing "non-value-added" work.) After documenting all preliminary ideas, the team estimated savings from each policy and identified short-, medium-, and long-term goals. A third group ultimately carried out implementation: it planned the redesign of the shop and set the implementation schedule.

This is when the problems started. Management had expected smooth sailing because of the work force's flexibility. As one manager recalled: "When we decided to introduce JIT and SPC, we talked with others who had already implemented them to learn from their experiences. They all said you get increased commitment from employees. And they did not have as highly flexible work situations as we did." But as JIT and SPC began to take hold, employees began to complain that the plant's basic principle of employee involvement was being undermined.

In fact, workers were losing much of their freedom with the regimentation necessitated by JIT and SPC. Particularly vexing was the elimination of buffer inventory between, and within, work teams. Many workers and team managers began to voice concern: "We're losing our team identity and individual freedom with JIT." "Management is reverting to the traditional control mentality." "The shift in the plant is from a human focus toward more business basics for survival."

In retrospect, it is hard to believe that none of us saw this coming. True, under JIT and SPC, employees become more self-managing than in a command-and-control factory. They investigate process improvements and monitor quality themselves; they consequently enjoy immediate, impartial feedback regarding their own performance. (Managers don't have to tell them how they're doing. They help design the system, and *it* tells them how they're doing.) They also gain a better understanding of all elements of the manufacturing process.

On the other hand, the reform process that ushers in JIT and SPC is meant to *eliminate all variations within production* and therefore requires strict adherence to rigid methods and procedures. With JIT, workers meet set cycle times; with SPC, they must follow prescribed problem-solving methods. In their pure forms, then, JIT and SPC can turn workers into extensions of a system no less demanding than a busy assembly line. They can push workers to the wall.

Let us look more closely at what is lost.

Loss of individual autonomy. In a continuous-process operation, the coupling of worker and machine is limited by *machine* cycle time. Operators typically have a significant period to monitor dials or gauges, which may allow them a certain amount of slack time. Similarly, lengthy machine cycles often provide operators sufficient time to perform "vertical" tasks (administrative or other duties traditionally performed by supervisors or staff personnel) or to assemble for a team meeting.

In a nonautomated or barely automated assembly line, the limiting factor is *operator* cycle time. With JIT, buffers are reduced—as is slack and idle time. As a result, employees have less time, if any, for vertical tasks or team meetings. Operators in job shops, who are expected to run multiple machines, can conceivably have even less time than workers in assembly line operations.

Although JIT advocates argue that abolishing wasteful operations leads to more meaningful, effective work, there are in fact a number of reasons for higher stress levels among line operators under JIT. Under the Toyota Production System, for example, workers adhere to rigid cycle times and are expected to adjust immediately to changes as demand fluctuates.

At Toyota, a multiskilled operator attends to as many as 16 machines at once. The operator first picks up one unit brought from the preceding process and sets it on the first machine. At the same time, he (or she) detaches another piece already processed by this machine and puts it on a chute in front of the next machine. Then, while walking to the second machine, he pushes a switch to start the first machine. After performing a similar sequence on all 16 machines, the operator returns to the initial process. "This is done in exactly the cycle time necessary, perhaps five minutes, so one unit of a finished gear will be completed in five minutes."[1]

According to one informed observer, line operators at Toyota have claimed that the JIT pace led to "more major accidents (resulting in a loss of four or more days at work) than in other Japanese automakers and an unusually high number of suicides among the blue-collar work force." Officials deny such claims but do admit that they encountered startup problems: lack of skills in adjusting to different types of equipment and resistance to running multiple machines.[2] Incidentally, less severe but similar problems occurred at the engine plant, where there was an increase in the number of medical restrictions for working on the assembly line under JIT.

At the engine plant, finally, the inflexible pace of the line impaired motivation. As one manager commented: "Everyone is affected. If I were a person who liked to build a lot of engines and could work fast, the line used to be fun. It felt good, I accomplished a lot, and got a lot of satisfaction from it. Today, I am slowed down and bored. Or take a slow person, one who wasn't pushed

at all by the old system. He would now have an awful lot of stress because he's really pacing the line. The entire day is very stressful."

Loss of team autonomy. Under JIT, individual team activities must be tightly coordinated with other teams in the production pipeline.

Collaboration among work teams protects workers' self-esteem.

The loss of inventory buffers means that team meetings cannot simply be held whenever the need arises. Even coffee breaks must be coordinated across teams. As a result, individual team autonomy is replaced by carefully structured patterns of collaboration. Which is why team members at the engine plant complained that they had less freedom in solving problems; they felt limited in making process improvements because they believed they could only make changes that didn't affect other teams.

In addition, JIT drastically alters performance measurements. In traditional line flows, team members are typically given monthly stretch goals, as opposed to daily quotas. Under JIT, performance is measured against cycle goals. "It is not a 30-day time span, it is a 3-minute time span," noted one manager. Another put it this way: "It used to be that you had a monthly goal and you really shot for it. If you were down, you would have the business manager and the team manager—everyone working on the line—try to make the monthly goal. Now they have targets every day. It used to be that you could loaf a little bit, and other days you knew you were under the gun. Now you're under the gun all the time."

Loss of autonomy over methods. When the engine plant first started, teams had a great deal of autonomy in the improvement process. They

had the freedom, within certain guidelines, to make changes on a trial basis; they were encouraged to be free-lancers, to take risks. As one team manager noted: "I was told in strong terms during the first several years I was here that I wasn't to do anything just because 'that's the way it's done.' I was told to do things the smartest way I could." Under JIT and SPC, this "entrepreneurial" spirit was limited; ideas are still encouraged but have to be tested under SPC guidelines.

Clearly, managers shouldn't give license to experiment where, in departing from established procedures, workers might jeopardize product integrity. But displacing worker trial and error with more scientific methods may have a negative psychological effect. Employees complained that SPC's structured experimentation restricted their freedom to make process changes. They perceived a loss of trust. As one manager noted: "It used to be that workers trusted us to listen to their ideas. Now we are troubleshooting more analytically and saying 'no' to workers more often than not. We say that their ideas don't fit SPC procedures. They say their ideas used to be worth something—now they are not."

Finally, SPC's process-capability studies may require operator certification programs. This is demoralizing for veteran workers. One worker responded to the certification process this way: "I can run every machine on this line, and I have done it on weekends, holidays, whenever. Now you say that I have to pass this road test to do it."

From autonomy to collaboration

What is to be done? Obviously, worker participation programs were never a carte blanche issued to operators to run production processes the way they wanted. The programs recognized axioms like concern for the customer, for the next team on the line, and for the schedule. Indeed, under JIT and SPC, tasks are more tightly coupled than ever before.

The key to protecting workers' self-esteem, then, is setting up a process for greater collaboration between teams—a time-consuming process, to be sure, but worth it in the long run. At NUMMI, the GM-Toyota joint venture, collaboration is now the name of the game. Whenever there is a cycle-time change (like when the plant went from a 54-second to a 68-second cycle time to accommodate slackening market demands), the teams have two to four weeks to plan changes in work station assignments. Teams have significant latitude in determining task sequences and work methods at each station; the team leaders (UAW working leaders) and group leaders (first-line supervisors) essentially become industrial engineers.

The objective is to balance the work load across all stations. This eliminates "cake jobs" and ensures that team members who rotate between stations within their teams can perform their tasks following standard procedures. When, for example, one team believes it would be better to reassign a particular task to another team—thereby changing the assembly sequence—all teams involved must reach a consensus.

Likewise, when a team member has a suggestion for improving a standardized job, a collaborative process begins again. The team member explains the idea to the team leader on that shift. If the team leader agrees that the idea has merit, the two try to sell it to their group leader. If the group leader likes it, then the three of them present it to the group leader and team leader on the other shift. Once there is a consensus at this level, the team members on both shifts are asked for input. If there is a problem, both shifts meet to try to gain consensus.

If there is agreement, the idea is ready for implementation. One shift will first try it out for approximately

one week. During this period, the team leader, group leader, and quality assurance personnel evaluate the change, making modifications where necessary. If the idea works, it's instituted across shifts.

Again, process may appear tedious, but both managers and team members agree that the system has mitigated the frustrations that workers are apt to feel in such an interdependent system. It pushes joint responsibility and ownership for goals and objectives down to the teams and encourages their members, who cannot be wholly responsible for problem solving and designing work methods, to at least feel like participants. Needless to say, this is a far cry from the previous traditional management style at GM plants, where engineers dictated the work methods.

The only decision at NUMMI that might be considered completely at the discretion of individual workers is the pulling of the "andon," or line stop cord. However, even this initiates a collaborative process: when the cord is pulled, the team leader

> ## Caution: The closer WIP inventory gets to zero, the more slack time you've eliminated.

and the group leader quickly converge on the troubled work station to help solve the problem.

Tektronix also chose to emphasize the need for collaboration, but in a less structured way. For the assembly of one of Tektronix's portable oscilloscopes, a team of 35 assemblers and technicians broke into four subgroups: three feeder groups channeling work via a kanban system to a final assembly group. Individuals were free to change the procedure at their own work station, provided it did not affect any other work station. The revised procedure sheet informed anyone filling in at that station of any changes. (If a change

affected the product in any way, the suggestion had to be reviewed with a team engineer.)

If any team member at Tektronix wanted to make a change that affected other members of the subgroup, for example, a change in the sequence of operations, the team member had to gain consensus from the group before making the change. If the change affected the entire team, however, the suggestion had to be raised at a weekly team meeting, where members would make a collaborative decision.

Here are other specific suggestions to mitigate the harsh effects of JIT and SPC:

Rethink zero inventory. In moving toward JIT, reducing inventory to an absolute zero level may not be the most economical or the wisest thing to do, at least not if it invites the system to break down.

The ultimate goal of JIT should be process control, not merely reducing inventory levels. NUMMI maintains a low level of "standard in-process stock" to balance the line and assure efficiency of the process. A minimum level of inventory may be justified to allow for team discussions or to alleviate individual employee stress. At the Saab-Valmet plant in Finland, for instance, buffers don't go below 20 minutes worth of work, because, as one of the managers put it, "Scandinavian respect for the workers' quality of life requires that the worker have the ability to work quickly for a few minutes in order to take a small personal break without stopping the line."[3]

Emphasize flow, not pace. Although JIT eliminates workers' ability to control their own work pace, using a kanban system allows workers to answer to each other rather than to a computer printout or supervisors. On the whole, kanban allows for more person-to-person initiative and communication. It therefore leads to a perception of increased worker control over the flow of production—though the reality may be otherwise. At Tektronix, for example, one team suggested increasing the kanban size to smooth

1. Yasuhiro Monden, *Toyota Production System: Practical Approach to Production Management* (Atlanta, Ga.: Industrial Engineering and Management Press, 1983), pp. 69-70.

2. Michael A. Cusumano, *The Japanese Automobile Industry: Technology and Management at Nissan and Toyota* (Cambridge: Harvard University Press, 1985), p. 305.

3. Suzanne de Treville, "Disruption, Learning, and System Improvement in Just-in-Time Manufacturing," unpublished dissertation, Harvard Business School, 1987.

production flow and still actually maintained daily output. If, however, too small a number of kanban squares allows for no buffer stock, the "human" system may prove even more stressful than any computerized one.

Focus on task design, not execution. Although there are limits on team freedom with respect to task execution, there is still room for

> ## Workers who choose when to rotate tasks will feel freer.

teams to be involved in task design. Teams can still have significant say regarding initial tooling and task sequence. Indeed, given the short product life cycles in many industries, production processes tend to be very dynamic; new products mean many new opportunities for employees to contribute to the work method. Of course, the excitement may wear off if the job becomes routinized over several months. It's important to allow for continual reassessment of the process.

Give workers the right to move and choose. As long as teams coordinate their activities with other teams, there is nothing to suggest that management must establish the times of breaks or "indirect" tasks. One might even argue that JIT and SPC give workers more opportunity to move around—to rotate between jobs or fill in wherever a problem arises. Such movement, of course, is not wholly discretionary. Workers must move where they are needed. Nevertheless, the sheer relief of changing tasks can make workers feel freer.

Furthermore, JIT and SPC do not restrict team autonomy with respect to assigning individual members to various tasks or determining job rotations. In some processes, team members may also be able to establish their own work hours, in accordance with a set flextime plan. At

Tektronix, the first assemblers to arrive will fill their kanbans; if the assemblers in the following work stations have not arrived, the first assemblers will then rotate to the next station, working down the line until others arrive.

Teams can have significant autonomy in laying out the job. The technology will, in part, dictate the parameters. However, in many cases a team could simply be given the square footage available and a blank piece of paper to design its space.

Allow for workplace management of quality and resources. JIT helps to uncover the "rocks"—the bottlenecks and wasted motion—and SPC provides a tool for improving quality. Team members should be encouraged to reject incoming nonconforming materials and halt outgoing shipments of poor-quality goods. Teams can also continue to control quality through peer evaluations in performance ratings.

Moreover, work teams typically have access to and responsibility for securing the resources they need for their production goals. They may monitor and disperse resources within budget constraints, make staffing decisions, train new team members, and obtain assistance from support personnel. JIT and SPC in no way limit overall team autonomy in these areas, only the timing of these activities.

Managers experienced with JIT and SPC establish set times when teams and team members can perform such activities. Moreover, vertical tasks can be rotated among individual team members when production pressures require workers full-time on the line. Team meetings can be held during shift overlaps or when the line is shut down.

All such ideas require revising traditional performance measurement systems. Companies recognize the need to schedule downtime for preventative maintenance of machines. But preventative maintenance for people is just as critical. Employees need periodic relief—more frequently than a scheduled ten-minute break every two hours—especially as cycle times shorten.

NUMMI plans for the line to be down 5% of the time as a result of line stops.

Managing expectations

If employees have never been given the latitude associated with self-managing work teams, their expectations tend to be lower. Hence many of the problems encountered by the engine manufacturer will not surface right away when JIT and SPC are introduced. But managers in high-commitment work systems particularly have to modify their workers' expectations without appearing to be reversing philosophy. This takes time. Time to teach, time to try to reach a consensus among workers that the changes associated with JIT and SPC are necessary.

As one manager at the engine manufacturer noted, "The teams feel like something was done to them, not with them. It is like having to get married, rather than wanting to get married." In the long run, a patient courtship will pay off.

> ## Why promise more autonomy when you mean workers to deliver more cooperation?

And aside from time, there is timing. If, for example, worker participation programs are implemented *after* JIT, there will be less confusion: workers will then not be invited to imagine greater freedom just when the new process takes freedom away. Even if some workers participate in the design of the system, this doesn't necessarily mean the plant will be operated by worker teams from the start. Besides, it is the task of managers, as always, to prepare the ground. They ought not to promise workers autonomy when they mean them to deliver an unprecedented degree of cooperation.

Reprint 89209

Doing away with the factory blues

When factory employees are given the same respect and concern usually shown only to office people, the results benefit both employees and management

Donald N. Scobel

When one thinks of a factory, images of a Dickensian sort often spring to mind: soot-coated windows, row upon row of down-trodden employees, and a stern, fat-bellied boss sitting in a window-office high above the work floor where no one can reach him. Although these stereotypes are no longer realities, and most factories are clean, healthy places in which to work, many plants are still inhospitable to most people. Is this situation unavoidable in a factory? In reporting on a new approach to revitalize the factory's work climate that is being carried out in some plants of Eaton Corporation, the author of this article says no. He asserts that by simply replacing many discriminatory personnel policies and practices which assume that the factory employee is untrustworthy and antiproductive and by instituting new ones, management can create a workplace where the aims of the business are congruent with the employees' desires for a happy work experience. The aim of the new approach is not to enrich employees' jobs, but rather to create a responsive work climate where desires for job enrichment can arise and be fulfilled along the way. The author also reports on how efforts to implement the new approach in older plants do meet with some resistance at first, but how it appears that they too will be successful.

Donald N. Scobel is manager of Employee Relations Research & Development at the Eaton Corporation. He has been with Eaton for almost twenty years and on the corporate staff for more than ten. The emerging processes and work climates described in this article occupy most of his efforts.

Reprint 75610

During the past few decades, the financial lot of the U.S. factory employee has been enhanced immeasurably by beneficial laws, organized and persuasive representation, economic clout, and, until recently, a generally increasing economy. The factory employee now also has more avenues than ever before to lodge specific protests and to achieve some social equity through grievance procedures, courts, labor boards, equality commissions, safety councils, and arbitration hearings.

Despite these social and economic advances for the factory employee, however, the factory itself has retained much of its classism and discrimination. Even with the dissections of academia, decades of behavioral science, theories of job enrichment and of human relations, new styles of management, and concepts of organizational development, the factory remains the kind of place nonfactorymen hope their children never have to work in as well as the kind of place factorymen hope their children can get out of. Why?

Why must the U.S. factory cause unhappiness for so many of its inhabitants? Why is it that an average of a few hundred people spending more than a third of their lives under a common roof cannot seem to find there a sustaining measure of equity, understanding, or even friendship? How can this mini-society called the workplace, where members are truly dependent on each other for economic security, remain so socially and emotionally sterile?

Part of the problem is that most people concerned with improving the lot of "people at work" fail to see the workplace holistically. Behavioral scientists, managements, unions, consultants, and legislators often concern themselves with separate segments of the industrial complex. Those who are concerned with styles of management do not worry about how the job is separate from the environment. Those concerned about worker alienation generally leave problems of the white collar force to others. Still other groups work to improve laws for the non-exempt. Yet these individual efforts rarely succeed in establishing a work culture where internal social values and business objectives are congruent.

In the past six years, however, considerable work has been done at several U.S. Eaton Corporation locations to provide the foundation for a workplace culture quite different from the more common industrial environment. At the outset, management did not form work teams, thrust a system of enriched jobs on the workplace, or even presume that the participation of people in decisions directly affecting them is a necessary ingredient of a healthy work culture. The thrust at the Eaton plants was simply for a climate of responsible industrial freedom, where the respect, dignity, and trust due a "man at work" is not culturally different from those due a man at church, a man bowling, or a man in tune with his own family. Management's effort was to achieve a happy, responsive work culture that would respond constructively to job enrichment, decision participation and involvement, or whatever grassroots needs, as they emerged.

The "Eaton story" may at times seem as if it were a fairy tale. Indeed, the approach used at Eaton has been spawned and nurtured more by innocence than by behavioral analysis, and that may have been part of its magic. Regardless, since 1968 about 13 Eaton manufacturing plants, involving over 5,000 people, have tried and succeeded in establishing a responsive workplace. Each plant's approach is tailored to the needs of its employees, which include foundry workers, truck transmission and axle makers, lift truck and auto parts makers, and forestry equipment and hardware builders.

It all began seven years ago when the manager of Eaton's Battle Creek, Michigan engine valve plant decided to build a new facility in Kearney, Nebraska. He asked his managerial staff and the Cleveland headquarters employee relations people how he might avoid the deterioration in employee/management relationships in Nebraska that had occurred over the decades in the Michigan plant.

In response to this challenge, a few managerial people representing the full spectrum of functional disciplines at Eaton isolated themselves to discuss and evaluate traditional policies and practices that affect employee relations. They summarized their composite critique in a report to the Battle Creek manager that took the form of a letter written as if by a factory employee who is explaining why he brings so little of himself to his workplace.

The employee's letter

Beginning in the Nebraska cornfields and spreading to other new facilities and, more recently, to some older plants, Eaton's revolt against the factory blues began with this "letter."

Dear Sir:

What you are asking me, as I see it, is why am I not giving you my best in exchange for the reasonable wages and benefits you provide me and my family.

First, I'm not trying to blame anybody for why you don't see the "whole" me. Some of the problem is company policy, some is union thinking, some is just me. Let me tell you why, and I'll leave it to bigger minds than mine to figure out blames and remedies.

I'll begin with my first day on the job eleven years ago—my first factory job, by the way. I was just 19 then. Incidentally, my cousin started work in your office as a clerk typist on the same day. We used to drive to work together. She still works for you, too.

The first thing I was told that day by the personnel manager and my foreman was that I was on 90 days' probation. They were going to measure my ability and attendance and attitude and then make up their minds about me. Gee, that surprised me. I thought I'd been hired already—but I really wasn't. Although the foreman tried to make me feel at home, it was still sort of a shock to realize I was starting out kind of on the sidelines until I proved my worth. In fact, the only person who told me I "belonged," without any strings attached, was my union steward.

You know, that first day my foreman told me all about the shop rules of discipline as if I were going

to start out stealing or coming to work drunk or getting into fights or horseplay. What made it even worse was when I later found out that no one told my cousin she was on probation. I asked her if she had seen the rules, and here it is eleven years later and she still doesn't know there are about 35 rules for those of us working in the factory.

What it boils down to is that your policies—yes, and the provisions of our union contract—simply presume the factoryman untrustworthy, while my cousin in the office is held in much higher regard. It's almost like we work for different companies.

After I had been here about eight months, a car hit my car broadside on the way to work. My cousin and I were both taken to the hospital right away and released several hours later. As soon as I was released by the hospital, I called the plant to tell them what happened. I couldn't get through to my foreman, so I told my tale to a recording machine. When my cousin didn't show up by nine o'clock, her boss got worried and called the house and then the hospital. When he found out my cousin had a broken arm and some cuts, but was basically okay, he sent for a taxi to take her home.

Both my cousin and I ended up missing four days' work. On each of the next three days, I called and told the tape recorder I would not be in. I never heard from anybody in the company and when I got back to work later that week, my supervisor said, "Sure glad to see you're okay . . . it's a shame you spoiled your perfect attendance record. . . ."

Sir, I don't come to work to be worried about by someone. But I have some difficulty understanding why, when I'm absent, nobody really cares. It seems as if the company's just waiting for me to do something wrong. When I got back to work from that car accident, you started getting another little chunk less from me. Does that sound crazy? Or does it seem selfish?

Sir, why must I punch a time clock? Do you think I'd lie about my starting and quitting times? Why must I have buzzers to tell me when I take a break, relieve myself, eat lunch, start working, go home? Do you really think I can't tell time or would otherwise rob you of valuable minutes? Why doesn't the rest room I must use provide any privacy? Why do I have to drive my car over chuck holes while you enjoy reserved, paved parking? Why must I work the day before and after a holiday to get holiday pay? Are you convinced I will extend the holiday into the weekend—while, by the way, my cousin is thought to have more sense than that?

I guess I'm saying that when you design your policies for the very few who need them, how do you think the rest of us feel?

Sir, do you really think I don't care or don't know what you think of me? If you are convinced of that, then you will never understand why I bring less than all of myself to my workbench.

You know, sir, in my eleven years, I've run all kinds of machinery for you, but your company has never even let me look at what the maintenance man does when he has to repair one of my machines. No one has ever really asked me how quality might be better or how my equipment or methods might be improved. In fact, your policies drum it into me good and proper that you really want me to stay in my place. And now, *you* want to know why *I* don't pour it on? Wow! Don't you realize that I may want to contribute more than you let me? I know the union may be responsible for some of this—but again, I'm trying to explain why, not whose fault it is.

You know, sir, I would like a more challenging job, but that isn't the heart of the matter, not for me at least. If there were a sense of dignity around here, I could not hold back the effort and ideas within me, even if my particular job was less than thrilling. Many of my buddies do not want a greater job challenge, but they do want their modest contributions respected.

You know, my neighbor is a real quiet, sweet old man who just retired from here last month. When I ask him how he sums up his life's work, he says—and I can almost quote him exactly—"A pretty good place to work—only thing that really bothered me was that warning I got 26 years ago for lining up at the clock two and one-half minutes early."

Well, sir, I suspect that 26 years ago, you may have corrected this quiet, nice guy for lining up early at your clock. But the price you paid was making him a "clock watcher" for 26 years. I wonder—was that warning all that necessary? Why couldn't you have just told him why lining up early isn't a good idea and then relied on him to discipline himself? I wonder.

It has been said, sir, that factory people look upon *profit* as a dirty word. I don't feel that way, but you know, it's almost as if *love* is the dirty word here.

Why don't I give my best? Well, I guess I have a kind of thermostat inside me that responds to your warmth. Do you have a thermostat inside you?

Very truly yours,

The company's answer

The above letter all but spells out its own solutions. The epilogue of the report to the Michigan manager said: "To avoid industrial decay, build a plant around the presumed correctness of the letter writer." And this is what the manager of the new plant in Nebraska, and all managers of new Eaton plants built since then, set out to do. Critical to solving inequities and problems cited in the letter is that management's commitment to the new approach be made explicit from the very beginning and that supervisors reexamine factory relationships.

The first steps

At the new Eaton plants, management puts out a written handbook in which it commits itself to a counseling rather than a rules-penalties process; to weekly departmental meetings where employee inputs are sought; to manager roundtables and an "open floor" concept; to a uniform office-factory

benefit system; and to a foundation of concern, trust, and participation. The handbook states that "... an important concept here is that people are individuals ... and a company must relate to uniqueness if there is to be a full measure of personal growth and contribution to organizational objectives. The emphasis is upon employee involvement in matters that affect him and sharing the responsibility for an effective operation. It's a mutual fulfillment."

What Eaton does in the formal training of supervisors under the new model is remarkably minimal. In a two-day seminar, the group of supervisors spends the first day just talking about why people work and what they want out of life. The consensus usually is that "we are all into this for pretty much the same reasons." The group invariably believes there are personal differences in motivational priorities, but does not believe these differences can be categorized for any class or group of employees, or that different categories of motivational factors are inherently more important. Although behavioral scientists have dissected this premise almost to death, it is true that most people desire a sense of community at work. Recognizing this fact helps supervisors and managers see that treating employees under the same roof with different value systems does not make much "human" sense.

During the second day of the seminar the supervisors review the basic components of the new approach and consider how that approach helps build a common value system of respect and participation. The reason training can be minimal is that the supervisor steps from the seminar into a workplace where the new commitments and ground rules are in effect immediately. Another plus is that it is not necessary to have "behavioral science superstars" to understand or apply the new approach. Supervisors of varying competencies are usually at ease with this approach after only brief exposure. Very few clamor for the old regimentation, or see it as essential to their ability to supervise. One supervisor simply said, "Nothing fancy about this. It's just being human with biblical roots." Eaton is trying to resurrect fairness through identifiable policy changes that are fundamentally fair.

Policy changes

Space prohibits listing all aspects of this new approach. In essence, personnel policies and presumptions that are based on mistrust and lack of care are discarded and replaced, where necessary, with ones that reflect concern and mutual respect. The following are a few examples of how this attitude is applied to actual policies and processes.

☐

At the new Eaton plants, the hiring process is a meaningful, two-way exchange, which replaces the structured interview and the more common "get-me-twelve-warm-bodies-by-Tuesday" factory-hiring syndrome. Applicants and their spouses are invited in small groups to an after-dinner "coffee" where the plant's products, processes, and philosophy are discussed. Both factory and office employees take the group on a plant and office tour and encourage the applicant to spend additional time in departments that seem most attractive to him. Personnel people ask the newcomer to express his job preferences within his general skill level for initial placement or for later transfer if there is no opening in the department he selects. The people conducting the tour introduce the applicant to people he may be working for and with. With this open review of the job, the job seeker ends up knowing more about the company and its people than they do about him. This process extends to a drill press operator or a file clerk the concern and dignity that industry usually extends only to its applicants for managerial posts.

☐

There is no probationary period. Supervisors evaluate individually any problem that might arise with a new person. Although it can happen that supervisors may have to let someone go, the policy presumes that people are eager to work and to be dependable employees, rather than the opposite.

☐

The plants do not use time clocks, buzzers, or similar controls. Although the company needs records of time allocations for many legal as well as good business reasons, it assumes that individuals can accurately record their own times.

☐

The dual value system mentioned by the "letter writer" no longer exists. Many companies, including Eaton, have traditionally maintained reasonable, responsible relationships with their office and supervisory staffs and have solved problems with these employees by carefully appraising the facts of each case, counseling employees according to individual circumstances, and assuming that the employees are able to direct themselves rather than relying on a rigid penalty schedule for correcting behavior. This approach is now being used for all factory employees who once were subjected to a formal disciplinary system that had numerous posted rules and a sliding scale of penalties that went with them.

☐

All factory and office people also share the same benefit package. Levels of certain benefits vary with salary, but the system is uniform. Payment for casual absence is often a dynamic distinguisher between office and factory status. At the newer Eaton facilities, all people are paid for both casual and long-term absences and are under the same pay system for long-term absences.

☐

Office and factory supervisors hold departmental meetings at least once every two weeks to discuss issues that the employees themselves raise. Often the supervisor will have an employee lead the discussion.

☐

The plant manager chairs a periodic roundtable with representatives from all office and factory departments who are selected in whatever way the department decides. The participants prepare the agenda of concerns and the minutes, as well as post follow-up action notices on central and departmental bulletin boards.

☐

An "open floor" concept replaces the old "open door" policy. The "open door" implied to a factoryman, "If you want to do business with a staff person, you must come up to his front office." The new approach makes the factoryman's workplace as important an "office" as anyplace else in the facility. So that territorial barriers are specifically torn down,

the personnel department and other staff people make a point of conducting business at the employee's workplace as well as at their own.

☐

In a variety of ways, factory, supervisory, and lower-level office people participate in managerial meetings and functions. For example, the manager invites some factory and office people to his weekly staff meetings. Similarly, there is regular factory representation at production planning meetings, as well as factory participation on methods, products, and process engineering committees.

☐

At some locations, factory and lower-level office people are editors of the plant's newssheets. Often the recreational, social, and community affairs activities are independently managed, including direction of the fiscal aspects, by joint committees of factory and office people. Special committees (little ad hocracies) are formed from time to time to handle contingencies.

☐

It is common for factory people to volunteer to be plant tour guides, to be involved with food service, plant safety, and fire protection matters, even to the extent of codirection of these activities.

I hope the above list gives the reader some idea of what Eaton is trying to do. In addition to these items, there are two important kinds of experiences that flow from this approach. For employees who want them, there are opportunities to be involved in developing the scope of their jobs or in increasing their participation in decision making.

Job involvement

From the beginning of the workplace renaissance, Eaton has not tried to implement new work structures or process designs. Each of the newer plants began with updated versions of the same basic technologies and procedures used at its older counterparts. Management wanted first to restructure the work climate and then to be responsive to spontaneous employee drives for greater job involvement as these drives emerged. What followed clearly, and almost quantifiably, resulted from the new work culture.

In the new plants, almost all employees seek better and more rapid performance inspection and feedback. In some cases, some of the inspection duties have been taken over by the employees themselves and blended into their own manufacturing responsibilities and operations. Interestingly, until people achieve job proficiency, they want guidance on how to improve their performance.

About one third of the people seek some involvement in their equipment repair. A significant number do not seek this enrichment, but for those who do, it is meaningful, and most maintenance people are willing trainers. Although maintenance time does sometimes rise briefly, it soon goes down, and preventive maintenance practices become more routine.

On the average, three quarters of the factory employees want to learn more about the whole production process, and those familiar with the process sequence soon develop an "early alert" system that warns them of trouble elsewhere on the line. Often these employees ask for temporary reassignment to help resolve the production holdups. It is startling how quickly employees become familiar with the total manufacturing process and how many of them aid the supervisor in product flow planning and problem solving.

Almost a third of the work force diagnoses its own job methods and scopes. At one plant, a janitor persuaded his boss that he, rather than the purchasing department, could order local cleaning supplies because he would give it higher priority than they would. He was allowed to do so, while other janitors wanted no part of the telephoning and paper work. At another plant the lathe operators insisted they be allowed to join a meeting of equipment engineers to learn why their lathes were malfunctioning. Many times people come forth with combinations of jobs or changes in sequences that can improve output. Some improvements require that the job and pay structure be changed, but many can be accommodated by the existing system.

These experiences in job involvement result from a specific policy of laissez-faire. Management responds positively to involvement but does not attempt to structure it.

Participation in decision making

It is integral to many aspects of the new approach that employees should participate in decisions. This extends to specific decisions that affect work and the work life. For example, if a plant is on a two-shift, five-day operation, and business expands, the different departments will discuss different work-schedule options, such as weekend work, extended daily hours, or a third shift that could be used to handle the increase. Often management will express its thoughts and invite reactions; more often, the options are put to a vote. In either case, employee inputs are specifically invited before any decision is made.

At one plant several employees suggested the company try a four-day week. The suggestion was put to a vote—and passed; in another plant, it failed. Elsewhere, management asked the employees in one departmental unit to restructure their own job contents and assignments when the current system was obviously inequitable. At a few locations, employees have nominated and selected candidates for supervisory positions, and in one situation, the employees said another supervisor was not necessary!

Even in layoff circumstances, decision participation is invited. Although people do not like to vote on only negative alternatives, such as a reduction of the work force versus a reduction in working hours, if the company submits its preferred course to employee consideration, it will often find the attitudinal "pulse" and more often than not receive ideas for policy redirection. During one temporary layoff, plantwide discussion brought forth more layoff volunteers than were needed! In almost all cases, when the employees participate in decisions, they cooperate to the full with the final decision. As one manager put it, "I can no longer conceive of making a decision of major impact on any segment of that work force without first inviting meaningful dialogue."

The response

Although some problems have arisen under the new approach (I will discuss these below), nothing so far indicates that the basic concepts are off the mark. In fact, there are some interesting comparisons that can be drawn between the new model facilities and the older plants, indicating that the new approach increases both productivity and worker satisfaction.

Measures of success

At the new plants, absenteeism (casual as well as sick leaves) ranges from 0.5% to 3%, compared with 6% to 12% at traditional locations. Turnover is similarly reduced. With the new approach, voluntary

separations average under 4% annually, compared with up to 60% at traditional plants.

In the new plants the hourly product output (for identical blueprints of products run on similar equipment) will range from parity to 35% more than at the traditional plants. Of more importance to Eaton, however, is the longer range performance where trends are comparable. Management in the new locations actually hopes that productivity will fall off at times. A dip in productivity indicates that improvements are being made in the manufacturing process, which will lead to greater gains in the long run. It is interesting that some new locations report up to 15% less scrap and rework costs. Nevertheless, those plants that have the highest output gains report the least savings (if any) in the quality area. Most report reduced maintenance costs per unit of output once start-up problems are resolved.

On the other hand, new facilities often have a worse plant safety record than the older plants. Management speculates that this decline in safety is caused partly by the new work force's unfamiliarity with industrial hazards and by the fact that carelessness creeps in when people strive so hard to increase production. In any event, the safety problem has led employees to involve themselves more in plant and departmental safety activities.

Actions speak louder than words
These measurements are interesting, but are subject to all the problems involved in accurately compar-

ing even seemingly like facilities. Although many of the plants compared are "paired" in terms of product and basic machinery, there are crucial differences, such as age of equipment; length of production runs; availability and quality of raw materials, parts and supplies; climate; and reliance on a parent plant for services. These differences make it difficult to isolate and measure the involvement and effectiveness of people. One can tell what is happening at the new plants and what the work force's effect is on productivity more by examining actual events than by measuring output.

☐
At one plant an employee literally broke in to go to work. The first day his shift went to ten hours, requiring a 5:00 A.M. starting time, he arrived at 3:30 A.M., as was his usual habit of showing up an hour and a half early. Finding the whole place dark, unoccupied, and locked, and even though he lived nearby and could have returned home until the plant officially opened, he climbed a fence, pried open a window, turned on the lights, cleaned his area, and started up the heating equipment to warm his "plating" bath.
☐
At another facility, a significant number of day-shift people, while taking the family out for an evening "Dairy Queen," stop by the plant just to make sure everything is going all right on the night shift.
☐
A plant manager at one of the older plants visited a new model facility and wrote in his report to a vice-president, "... I'd sum it up by reporting that when the first shift ended you couldn't tell it was quitting time! No clocks to line up at! No rushing to cars! No tires screeching! Some people finished the last piece in their machine. Many casually took showers. Some went out to the picnic area and gossiped over a bottle of pop. Several stayed to play baseball or horseshoes in the back field. Some went to a variety of committee meetings. The point is that the exodus was so gradual it went unnoticed. Unbelievable!"
☐
A group of employees, on their own time, used company materials to build a special scooter to enable an employee who had become permanently handicapped in an automobile accident to return early to his job.
☐
At a facility where overtime work is assigned on a voluntary basis, for three months 97% of the people worked seven days a week with less than 2% absen-

teeism *during* the week, even though casual week-day absence would have been paid for.

☐

There have been no employee-initiated EEO or OSHA complaints at any facility where this approach to employee relationships is practiced.

☐

At a southern plant where 30% of the work force is black, the factory people selected five supervisors; three of them were black.

☐

Although there are not many transfers between office and factory positions, it is just as common to have office people apply for transfer to the factory as the other way around. At one plant, five office people volunteered to run factory machinery so five avid deer hunters could catch the first day of the season!

☐

At one location, a high-ranking visitor reported, among other things, "... the most remarkably constructive graffiti I have ever read ... the few cartoons, poems and song parodies are genuinely witty and poignant and prideful. What a difference from the traditional back walls of industry!"

☐

One New Year's Day, almost all the employees at one plant responded to a TV news bulletin that the plant was within an unexpected flood area. Most labored around the clock so the plant could be fully operational the next day.

☐

At one plant, if at the begining of his shift an employee registers his choice of lunch food, he will have a tray waiting for him at lunchtime. A cafeteria employee who thinks that "people's lunch break should be spent eating and gabbing and not waiting in line or kicking a vending machine" introduced the idea and carried it out.

These examples show how the new approach affects employees at work, and were perhaps best summarized by one manager when he said, "On those especially frustrating days I still know in my bones that nothing intentionally destructive is going on around here."

Problems of implementation

Although the humanistic approach to employee relationships has not failed at any location, there have, nevertheless, been growing pains. With vary-ing degrees of severity, most of the following problems have occurred at one or more plants.

Initially, Eaton concentrated its effort on employee relations in the factory. Although very few office people were averse to bringing dignity and fairness to the factory employees, when the factories were filled with camaraderie, the office people became envious of the "feeling." The office people did not have the sense of involvement with their workplace that management had assumed they did, and once the issue was raised it was clear why. Some plant managers did not include the office people in their roundtable discussions, and when they did conduct departmental meetings, which was infrequently, the meetings seemed pallid in comparison to factory meetings.

Management in the new plants solved these problems by stressing participation in the offices and ensuring more meaningful interaction between the office and factory employees so that all could share the same work climate. What Eaton had seen originally as a factory revitalization now involves the entire workplace.

Another related problem is what Eaton now calls the "up-the-ladder" disease. The first symptom appeared at a retreat that the manager of the new Nebraska plant held so that the supervisors could talk in a relaxed atmosphere about how things were going. This quasi-recreational gathering turned out to be a pressure cooker for the plant manager. The supervisors said most discreetly that their relationships with the factory employees were more spirited and participative than their rapport with higher management. They felt they were "short circuited" up the hierarchy. The plant manager realized he would have to be more awake and responsive to his supervisors and their ideas. Invariably, the cure for this disease is exposing higher management levels to the plant culture itself.

At one very small location, the plant manager ignored the espoused policies. The hiring orientation process fell short of the commitment, and departmental meetings did not occur. In reacting angrily to an employee soliciting money for his "cause," a department manager ignored individualized consideration and posted a mass denouncement on the bulletin board. As was immediately evident from the horrendous absentee and turnover experience, the managers were not treating the employees with respect and dignity. Luckily, the plant manager recognized what was happening and called the work force together to admit the hypocrisy and to pledge a speedy "new beginning," which has taken place.

There are different problems that arise when things go almost too smoothly. At a few places, for instance, the sense of goodwill was so pervasive that the company did not react to a few individuals who were exploiting the trust placed in them. The other employees became restless and brought pressure on these people directly as well as on management to deal with these individuals. In most cases, the peer pressure and counseling procedure has been effective, and the individuals responded positively.

Despite the implementation problems I have cited, the approach has been accepted in most new locations. Although not without its skeptics, the concept is now a familiar idea throughout the company, and many managers of traditional plants, which have varied histories of problems with factory and office employees, are searching out ways to apply the new approach at their own plants, where practices, policies, and attitudes are already firmly established.

The backward glance

Eaton's efforts at some older plants are still in early stages, and it is too soon to report significant successes or failures. It is already apparent, however, that remodeling is slower and more complex than building anew. It is equally evident, nevertheless, that meaningful changes can be made at traditional locations without great risk or investment. As at new locations, the company must express its commitment; the absence of commitment makes the ideas seem vague and philosophical rather than action oriented.

Understandably, it is much more difficult to convince supervisors, employees, and their unions in the older plants that change is not threatening and can take place with fairness and dignity. This task has become easier at Eaton since the word has now spread that the new plants are such fulfilling places to work in. It is still, however, a great challenge to managers in the traditional plants to bring everyone together without fanfare into a common constructive process, to get them to believe that management means what it is saying. If management tries to impose the new approach, it runs the risk of appearing as if it were just another management attempt to impose its will upon the employees. Because of these problems, managers in some older plants are using different approaches to attain the same ends.

At one old plant, there is a joint company-union initiated effort to transform the workplace climate through a variety of participative endeavors. These include such experiences as employees themselves rearranging an entire stockroom area more efficiently or management entrusting employees in a certain department with the responsibility of resolving their own absentee problems. At another location, the company has approached the union to recast the provisions of the labor agreement in language that assumes trust and respect between parties. The point is to see whether constructive relationships can emerge from changes in legalistic language and principles previously inscribed in stone.

More commonly, however, Eaton is trying to adapt its new plant experiences to traditional places. There is no theoretical reason that the new hiring procedure, the "open floor" policy, departmental meetings, the manager's roundtable, and the counseling approach to discipline cannot be initiated by managers in the plants. In fact, some of these changes are in process at older places and seem to attract voluntary union involvement and cooperation.

The union, of course, must be integrally involved in the entire change process. As management takes on a new role, so must the union and the employees. All three must involve themselves in some new processes that have them working together toward some common objectives. Working together seems to bring about change far sooner than does eons of dialogue.

From our early efforts to reduce alienation at traditional workplaces, it seems that decision participation must come into play early in the process. This comes slowly at first for people not accustomed to participating, but the encouragement to participate begins to narrow the credibility gap and most people join in after a few invitations.

Lastly, management must discard traditional policies and practices that presume or embody mistrust. Where these policies are rooted in provisions of a labor agreement such as the probationary concept or a host of other rigid systems, the company and union must work these out together. And this teamwork is not likely to occur unless the union and employees are playing a part in the entire change process.

P.S.

What Eaton is doing is not complex. When one observer suggested we were only getting the "Hawthorne effect," we glowed and said that was exactly right. All we are trying to do is "bottle" the Hawthorne effect, and share respect and concern with employees.

It is significant that about a quarter of the companies that research the Eaton approach and visit a facility adapt some form of the process for one or more of their own locations. Of equal significance, however, are some of the reasons cited by those who do not make changes in their own organizations. In some cases, the inquirer is personally enthusiastic but sees no chance to influence traditional higher management in his company. This happens mostly with people from small companies where the chief executive officer is seen as having a negative attitude that dominates the entire organization. In larger, multiple plant facilities, such as Eaton, the change is often introduced at an interested branch, and then spreads throughout the organization.

Conversely, in some cases the chief executive officer, impressed by the concept, expresses doubt that other key people in his organization could implement these new processes.

Some people say they are hesitant to propose such an approach in their own companies because there are so many seemingly complex theories of behavior now on the shelf that the company fears embarking on any particular course when it may soon be outdated. Some inquirers are actually startled to find that Eaton people are not steeped in any particular behavioral school.

Those companies that have tried the Eaton approach have confirmed our experiences. They report:

1
This approach is fundamentally fair and makes sense even if it doesn't prove to be a panacea.
2
It is based on some very specific and simple actions that can be implemented by existing personnel.
3
The company can rely on its own innovators, and not, as one inquirer put it on "a behavioral guru."
4
The approach does not require a large financial investment, and even a 1% increase in plant utilization or a 2% drop in absenteeism brings a substantial return on investment.

At Eaton we are convinced that concern, respect, and trust in people produce a cohesive and effective workplace. Complex evaluation procedures, behavioral science theories and analyses, job design, and individual consultations are not primary and often not necessary. In fact, the process is more akin to an attitude than to a detailed intellectual plan. Most supervisors and managers boast of the esprit de corps and excitement that builds as the approach takes hold. One manager, when asked by a visitor just beginning his tour, "What will I see different out there?" responded, "A feeling."

Perhaps behavioral science's gallop is leaping over some very simple and moving truths. When bird hunters spontaneously prepare a duck casserole luncheon for the entire work force; when a fifty-seven-year-old-man boasts how his wife of thirty-seven years has finally got him bowling and dancing " 'cause I come home so rarin' "; when a plant's annual aspirin consumption is down to a small bottle; when hospitalized employees are visited by about 20% of the work force; when the plant community spontaneously plants trees and shrubs to create its own wooded picnic area; and when a guitar-playing employee sits in that picnic area and sings his own folk song about a "workplace havin' soul," then something constructive and productive is truly happening somehow.

Pay and Performance

The attack on pay

Rosabeth Moss Kanter

Status, not contribution, has traditionally been the basis for the numbers on employees' paychecks. Pay has reflected where jobs rank in the corporate hierarchy—not what comes out of them.

Today this system is under attack. More and more senior executives are trying to turn their employees into entrepreneurs—people who earn a direct return on the value they help create, often in exchange for putting their pay at risk. In the process, changes are coming into play that will have revolutionary consequences for companies and their employees. To see what I have in mind, consider these actual examples:

☐ To control costs and stimulate improvements, a leading financial services company converts its information systems department into a venture that sells its services both inside and outside the corporation. In its first year, the department runs at a big profit and employees begin to wonder why they can't get a chunk of the profits they have generated instead of just a fixed salary defined by rank.

☐ In exchange for wage concessions, a manufacturer offers employees an ownership stake. Employee representatives begin to think about total company profitability and start asking why so many managers are on the payroll and why they are paid so much.

☐ To encourage initiative in reaching performance targets, a city government offers large salary increases to managers who can show major departmental improvements. After a few years, the amount in managers' paychecks bears little relationship to their levels in the organization.

In traditional compensation plans, each job comes with a pay level that stays about the same

Ms. Kanter is the Class of 1960 Professor of Business Administration at the Harvard Business School. She has written numerous books, including Men and Women of the Corporation (Basic Books, 1979) and The Change Masters: Innovation and Entrepreneurship in the American Corporation (Simon & Schuster, 1983). Her HBR article "Power Failure in Management Circuits" (July-August 1979) won that year's McKinsey Award.

regardless of how well the job is performed or what the real organizational value of that performance is. Pay scales reflect such estimated characteristics as decision-making responsibility, importance to the organization, and number of subordinates. If there is a merit component, it is usually very small. The surest way—often the only way—to increase one's pay is to change employers or get promoted. A mountain of tradition and industrial relations practice has built up to support this way of calculating pay.

> ## Reward performance you want to encourage.

Proponents of this system customarily assert that the market ultimately determines pay, just as it determines the price of everything else that buyers wish to acquire. Compensation systems cannot be unfair or inappropriate, therefore, because they are incapable of causing anything. Actually, however, because it is so difficult to link people's compensation directly to their contributions, all the market really does is allow us to assume that people occupying equal positions tend to be paid equally and that people with similar experience and education tend to be worth about the same. So while the market works in macroeconomic terms, the process at a microeconomic level is circular: we know what people are worth because that's what they cost in the job market; but we also know that what people cost in the market is just what they're worth.

Given logic like this, it's not hard to see why such strange bedfellows as feminist activists and entrepreneurially minded managers both attack this traditional system as a manifestation of the paternalistic benefits offered across the board by Father Corporation. "We've got corporate socialism, not corporate capitalism," charged the manager of new ventures for a large industrial company. "We're so focused on consistent treatment internally that we destroy enterprise in the process."

These old arrangements are no longer supportable. For economic, social, and organizational reasons, the fundamental bases for determining pay are under attack. And while popular attention has focused on comparable worth—equalizing pay for those doing comparable work—the most important trend has been the loosening relationship between job assignment and pay level.

Four separate but closely related concerns are driving employers to rethink the meaning of worth and look beyond job assignments in determining pay—equity, cost, productivity, and the rewards of entrepreneurship.

It's not fair!

Every year, routine company surveys show fewer employees willing to say that traditional pay practices are fair. In particular, top management compensation has been assailed as unjustifiably high, especially when executives get large bonuses while their companies suffer financial losses or are just recovering from them.

Despite economic data showing an association between executive compensation and company performance, many professionals still argue that the amounts are excessive and reflect high status rather than good performance. Likewise, the existence of layers on layers of highly paid managers no longer seems entirely fair. Employees question why executives should be able to capture returns others actually produce. And they are beginning to resent compensation plans like the one in a leading well-run bank that gives managers bonuses of up to 30% of their pay for excellent branch performance, while branch employees get only a 6% to an 8% annual increase.

If executives get bonuses for raising profits, many urge, so should the workers who contribute to those profits. Indeed, this is the theory behind profit sharing in general. Such programs, and there are several widely used variants, have in common the very appealing and well-accepted notion that all employees—not just management—should share in the gains from enhanced performance.

Profit sharing is ordinarily a straightforward arrangement in which a fraction of the net profits

Author's note: I thank Barry Stein, Cynthia Ingols, Paul Loranger, Carolyn Russell, Wendy Brown, and D. Quinn Mills for their valuable contributions.

from some period of operation are distributed to employees. The distribution may be either immediate or deferred, and the plan may not include all employees.

The plan at Lincoln Electric, the world's largest manufacturer of arc-welding products, is particularly generous. Every year, Lincoln pays out 6% of net income in common stock dividends—the "wages of capital." The board determines another sum to be set aside as seed money for investment in the future. The balance, paid to all employees, ranges from 20% of wages and salary, already competitive, to more than 120%. The company has remained profitable even in the face of sales declines in the 1981-1983 recession, to the benefit of employees as well as stockholders.

Overall, probably about a half million companies have some form of profit sharing, if both deferred and cash payouts are included. In private enterprises other than those categorized as small businesses, government statistics show that by 1983 19% of all production employees, 27% of all technical and clerical employees, and 23% of all professional and administrative employees were covered by profit-sharing agreements.

The variant known as gain sharing takes profit sharing one giant step further by attempting, usually with some elaborate formula, to calculate the contributions of specific groups of employees whose contingent pay depends on those varying results. Although the basis for calculation varies from one gain-sharing plan to another, the plans have two principles in common: first, the payout reflects the contribution of groups rather than individuals (on the theory that teams and collective effort are what count), and second, the rewards to be shared and the plan for their distribution are based on objective, measurable characteristics (so that everyone can see what is owed and when).

According to experts, several thousand companies have gain-sharing programs of some sort. These programs already involve millions of workers and seem to be growing in popularity. The Scanlon Plan, probably the oldest, best-known, and most elaborate gain-sharing system, usually distributes 75% of gains to employees and 25% to the company. In addition, this plan is organized around complex mechanisms and procedures that spell out how employees at various levels are to participate, not only in control of the process but also in opportunities to help improve performance and thereby their own shares. At Herman Miller, Inc., gain sharing is described not simply as a compensation system but rather as a way of life for the company.

Group or all-employee bonuses, especially when linked to fairly specific indicators, provide another way to share some of the benefits of good performance more equitably. But evidence shows that their potential far exceeds their use. Although group performance bonuses are continuing to grow, top executives are much more likely to capture a portion of the benefits of increased profitability than employees are. In a recent Conference Board study of 491 companies, 58% had top executive bonus plans but only 11% had profit-sharing plans, 8% all-employee bonuses, 3% group productivity incentives, and fewer than 1% group cost-control incentives.

Performance-related compensation plans generally ignore employees other than top management and, to a lesser extent, some middle managers. And even in incentive-conscious high-technology companies, gain sharing is rare. While more than half the high-tech companies included in a recent Hay Associates compensation survey had cash or stock awards for individuals, only 6% had gain-sharing or group profit-sharing programs. Concerns about equity – including those framed in terms of comparable worth – are not altogether misplaced therefore.

Companies have long been concerned with one fundamental fairness issue – the relative compensation of employees in general. Now, however, they face two new issues that are complex, hard to resolve, and rapidly getting worse. The first, evident in the debate over gain sharing and profit sharing, sets up what employees get against what the organization gets from their efforts. The second, evident in the debate over comparable worth, is how groups in an organization fare in relation to each other. At the very least, these issues call for better measurement systems or new principles on which various constituencies can agree.

Let them eat dividends

Facing challenges from competitors, companies in every field are seeking ways to reduce fixed labor costs. One sure way is to peg pay to performance – the company's as well as the individual's. Merit awards, bonuses, and profit-sharing plans hold out the promise of extra earnings for those who truly contribute. But it is their cost-reduction potential that really makes executives' eyes sparkle with dollar signs.

Making pay float to reflect company performance is the cornerstone of MIT economist Martin L. Weitzman's proposal for a "share economy." If many companies can be induced to share profits or revenues with their employees, Weitzman argues, then the cure for stagflation would be at hand. Among other things, companies would have an incentive to create jobs because more workers would be paid only in proportion to what they have brought in.[1]

For organizations struggling to compete, these macroeconomic implications are a lot less tanta-

lizing than the more immediate benefits to be gained by asking workers to take their lumps from business cycles – or, employees would add, poor management decisions – along with their companies. Moreover, a similar logic clearly accounts for some of the appeal of employee ownership, especially to companies in industries where deregulation has created enormous cost competitiveness.

According to one recent book about employee ownership, *Taking Stock: Employee Ownership at Work*, at least 6 major airlines and 15 trucking companies have adopted employee ownership plans in response to deregulation.[2] Overall, the authors estimate that some 11 million employees in 8,000-plus businesses now own at least 15% of the companies employing them.

While many companies have found employee ownership attractive primarily as a financing scheme, there is little doubt that, properly designed and managed, it can positively affect corporate success. Take Western Air Lines as an illustration. After losing $200 million over four years, this company created the Western Partnership by trading a 32.4% ownership stake, a meaningful profit-sharing plan, and four seats on the board of directors for wage cuts and productivity improvements of 22.5% to 30%. In 1985 Western distributed more than $10 million to its 10,000 employees – $100 each in cash and the rest in employees' accounts. Now employees are making about $75 million on Western's sale to Delta.

Such schemes have obvious advantages over another highly visible alternative for fixed-labor-cost reduction – two-tier wage systems, which bring in new hires at a lower scale than current employees. Most of us can see the obvious inequity in paying two groups differently for doing exactly the same job. But pay pegged to actual performance? Earnings tied to company profits? What could be more fair?

The clear problems – that lower paid employees cannot afford income swings as readily as the more highly paid and that employee efforts are not always directly related to company profitability – do not seem to deter the advocates. The fixed part of the paycheck is already shrinking in many American companies. Even the bonus is being used to supplement these efforts, especially among manufacturing companies. A recent study by the Bureau of National Affairs reveals that one-shot bonus payments, replacing general pay increases, were called for in almost 20% of all 1985 union contract settlements outside the construction industry, up from a mere 6% in 1984. Similarly, 20% of the 564 companies in Hewitt Associates' 1986

1 Martin L. Weitzman,
*The Share Economy:
Conquering Stagflation*
(Cambridge:
Harvard University Press, 1984).

2 Michael Quarrey, Joseph Blasi,
and Corey Rosen,
*Taking Stock:
Employee Ownership at Work*
(Cambridge, Mass.: Ballinger, 1986).

"Used to be sort of a Yuppy myself, but we called it 'up-and-comer.'"

compensation survey gave one-time bonuses to white-collar workers, up from 7% in 1985.

These one-time payments do not raise base pay, nor do they affect overtime calculations. In fact, just the opposite occurs: they reduce the cost of labor. More than two-thirds of the bonus provisions the BNA studied were accompanied by wage freezes or decreases.

Bucks for behavior

The cost attack is one straightforward way for companies to become more competitive, at least in the short run. In the long run, however, pay variations or rewards, contingent on specific and measurable achievements of individuals at every level, are likely to be even more effective in stimulating employee enterprise and channeling behavior. What better way could there be, proponents argue, to help employees recognize what is most useful and to guide their efforts appropriately?

Merrill Lynch's compensation system for its 10,400 brokers, introduced in February 1986, is a good example. To encourage brokers to spend more time with larger, more active customers, the firm has cut commissions for most small trades and discounts and rewards the accumulation of assets under its management. The pay system was developed in direct response to new products like the firm's Cash Manage-

ment Account because the old system wasn't adequate to reward performance in new and growing areas management wanted to stress.

Commissions and bonuses for sales personnel are standard practice in most industries, of course. What seem to be changing are the amounts people can earn (for example, more than double one's salary at General Electric Medical Systems' Sales and Service Division), the number of people who can earn them, and the variety of productivity bonuses, especially in highly competitive new industries.

PSICOR is a small Michigan company supplying equipment and professionals (called perfusionists) for open-heart surgery. Perfusionists are in great demand and frequently change employers, so founder Michael Dunaway searched for a way to give them immediate rewards because the standard 10% increase at the end of the year was too remote.

First he tried random bonuses of $100 to $500 for superior performance, but tracking proved difficult. Then in 1982 he hit on the idea of continuous raises—increases in every paycheck—calculated to add up to at least a 5% annual raise over base salary, with up to 8% more in a lump sum at year-end based on overall performance. Employee response was positive, but the accounting department was soon drowning in paperwork.

PSICOR's latest system combines quarterly raises of up to 5% a year, based solely on performance, with a series of additional bonuses to reward specific activities: higher caseloads, out-of-town assignments, professional certification, and the like. Turnover is less than 2% and drops to less than 1/2% for those employed two years or more.

Of course, some companies are going in exactly the opposite direction—for seemingly good reason. As an ex-director of sales compensation for IBM confessed, "We used to give bonuses and awards for every imaginable action by the sales force. But the more complex it got, the more difficult it was to administer, and the results were not convincing. When we began to ask ourselves why Digital Equipment had salespeople, who are tough competitors, on straight salary, we decided perhaps we'd gone overboard a bit."

Even in commercial real estate leasing, long a highly performance-oriented business, one major and very effective Boston company—Leggat, McCall & Werner, Inc.—has for years had its brokers on salary.

Nevertheless, the tide is moving in the other direction—toward more varied individual compensation based on people's own efforts. This trend reaches its fullest expression, however, not in pay-for-performance systems like those just described but in the scramble to devise ways to reward people in organizations for acting as if they were running their own businesses.

A piece of the action

The prospect of running a part of a large corporation as though it were an independent business is one of the hottest old-ideas-refurbished in American industry. Many companies are encouraging potential entrepreneurs to remain within the corporate fold by paying them like owners when they develop new businesses. And even very traditional organizations are looking carefully at the possibility of setting up new ventures with a piece of the action for the entrepreneurs. "If one of our employees came along with a proposition, I'm not sure how anxious we'd be to do it," one bank executive said. "But ten years ago, we wouldn't have listened at all. We'd have said, 'You've got rocks in your head.'"

Most of the new entrepreneurial schemes pay people base salaries, generally equivalent to those of their former job levels, and ask them to put part of their compensation at risk, with their ownership percentage determined by their willingness to invest. This investment then substitutes for any other bonuses, perks, profit sharing, or special incentives they might have been able to earn in their former jobs. Sometimes the returns are based solely on percentages of the profits from their ventures; sometimes the returns come in the form of phantom stock pegged to the companies' public stock prices. Potential entrepreneurs cannot get as rich under this system as they could if they were full owners of independent businesses who shared ownership with other venture capitalists. But they are also taking much less risk.

AT&T's new venture development process, begun just before divestiture, illustrates how large corporations are trying to capture entrepreneurship. Currently seven venture units are in operation, each sponsored by one of AT&T's lines of business. One started in 1983, three in 1984, and three more in 1985. The largest is now up to 90 employees.

William P. Stritzler, the AT&T executive responsible for overseeing this process, offers venture participants three compensation alternatives corresponding to three levels of risk.

Option one allows venture participants to stick with the standard corporate compensation and benefits plan and to keep the salaries associated with their previous jobs. Not surprisingly, none of the seven has chosen this option.

Under option two, participants agree to freeze their salaries at the levels of their last jobs and to forgo other contingent compensation until the venture begins to generate a positive cash flow and the AT&T investment is paid back (or, with the concurrence of the venture board, until the business passes certain milestones). At that point, venture participants can get one-time bonuses equal to a maximum of 150% of their salaries. Five of the seven venture teams have selected this option.

The third option, chosen by two self-confident bands of risk takers, comes closest to simulating the independent entrepreneur's situation. Participants can contribute to the venture's capitalization through paycheck deductions until the venture begins to make money and generate a positive cash flow. Investments are limited only by the requirement that salaries remain above the minimum wage – to avoid legal problems and prevent people from using personal funds. In exchange, participants can gain up to eight times their total investment.

To date, participants have put in from 12% to 25% of their salaries, and one of the two ventures has already paid several bonuses at a rate just below the maximum. The other, a computer-graphics-board venture housed outside Indianapolis, could return $890,000 to its 11 employee-investors in the near future.

The numbers show just how attractive AT&T employees find this program: ideas for new ventures began coming in before the program was announced, and in the planning year alone, 300 potential entrepreneurs developed proposals. Perhaps 2,000 ideas have been offered since, netting a venture formation rate of about 1 from every 250 ideas. People from every management level have been funded, including a first-line supervisor and a fifth-level manager (at AT&T, roughly equivalent to those just below officer rank), and in principle, management is even willing to offer this option to nonmanagers.

Entrepreneurial incentives are especially prevalent at high-technology companies – not surprising given the importance and mobility of innovators. For example, a 1983 random sample of 105 Boston-area companies employing scientists and engineers compared the high-tech enterprises, dependent on R&D for product development, with their more traditional, established counterparts. The high-tech companies paid lower base salaries on average but offered more financial incentives, such as cash bonuses, stock options, and profit-sharing plans.[3]

The entrepreneurial paycheck is on the rise wherever management thinks that people could do as well or better if they were in business for themselves – in high tech and no-tech alike. Au Bon Pain, a Boston-based chain of bakeries and restaurants, with $30 million in revenue from 40 stores nationwide, is launching

3 Jay R. Schuster,
*Management Compensation in
High Technology Companies:
Assuring Corporate Excellence*
(Lexington, Mass.: Lexington Books,
1984).

a partnership program that will turn over a big piece of the action to store managers. Under the plan, annual revenues exceeding $170,000 per store will be shared fifty-fifty with the partners.

If business developers and revenue growers are getting a chance to share in the returns, will inventors in the same companies be far behind? Probably not. The inventors' rights challenge is another nudge in the direction of entrepreneurial rewards.

Traditional practice has rewarded salaried inventors with small bonuses (often $500 to $1,000) for each patent received and some nonmonetary incentives to encourage their next inventions. Recognition ranges from special awards and promotion to master status entailing the use of special laboratories, freedom of project choice, sabbaticals, and the like. Cash awards are often given, but they are generally not tied to product returns. For outstanding innovation, IBM, for example, offers awards (which can be $10,000 or more) and invention achievement ($2,400 and up).

Increasingly, however, we are seeing strong competitive and legal pressures to reward employed inventors as if they were entrepreneurs by tying their compensation to the market value of their output. They too want a piece of the action and a direct return on their contributions.

The challenge to hierarchy

If pay practices continue to move toward contribution as the basis for earnings, as I believe they will, the change will unleash a set of forces that could transform work relationships as we know them now. To illustrate, let's look at what happens when organizations take modest steps to make pay more entrepreneurial.

In 1981, the city of Long Beach, California established a pay-for-performance system for its management as part of a new budgeting process designed to upgrade the city government's performance against quantifiable fiscal and service delivery targets. Under the new system, managers can gain or lose up to 20% of their base salaries, so the pay of two managers at the same level can vary by up to $40,000. Job category and position in the hierarchy are far weaker determinants of earnings. In fact, at least two people are now paid more than the city manager.

While the impact of a system like this on productivity and entrepreneurship is noticeable, its effect on work relationships is more subtle. People don't wear their paychecks over their name badges in the office, after all. But word does get around, and some

organizations are having to face the problem of envy head-on. In two different companies with new-venture units that offer equity participation, the units are being attacked as unfair and poorly conceived. The attackers are aggrieved that venture participants can earn so much money for seemingly modest or even trivial contributions to the corporation overall, while those who keep the mainstream businesses going must accept salary ceilings and insignificant bonuses.

> *The iron cage of bureaucracy is being rattled.*

In companies that establish new-enterprise units, this clash between two different systems is self-inflicted. But sometimes the conflict comes as an unwelcome by-product of a company's efforts to expand into new businesses via acquisition. On buying a brokerage firm, a leading bank found that it had also acquired a very different compensation system: a generous commission arrangement means that employees often earn twice their salary in bonuses and, once in a while, five times. In 1985, six people made as much in salary and commissions as the chairman did in his base salary, or roughly $500,000 each. These people all made much more than their managers and their managers' managers and virtually everyone else in the corporation except the top three or four officers, a situation that would have been impossible a few years ago.

Now such discrepancies cannot be prevented or kept quiet. "People in the trade know perfectly well what's happening," the bank's senior administration executive told me. "They know the formula, they see the proxy statements, and they are busy checking out the systems by which we and everybody else compensate these people."

To avoid the equivalent of an employee run on the bank—with everyone trying to transfer to the brokerage operation—the corporation has felt forced to establish performance bonuses for branch managers and some piece-rate systems for clerical workers, though these are not nearly as generous as the managers' extra earning opportunities.

This system, though it solves some problems, creates others. The executive responsible recognizes that although these new income-earning opportunities are pegged to individual performance, people do not work in isolation. Branch managers' results really depend on how well their employees perform, and so do the results of nearly everyone else except those in sales (and even there a team effort can make a difference). Yet instead of teamwork, the bank's practices may encourage competition, the hoarding of good leads, and the withholding of good ideas until one person can claim the credit. "We talk about teamwork at training sessions," this executive said, "and then we destroy it in the compensation system."

Team-based pay raises its own questions, however, and generates its own set of prickly issues. There is the "free rider" problem, in which a few nonperforming members of the group benefit from the actions of the productive members. And problems can arise when people resent being dependent on team members, especially those with very different organizational status.

> ## The new bottom line is what you contribute.

There are also pressure problems. Gainsharing plans, in particular, can create very high peer pressure to do well, since the pay of all depends on everyone's efforts. Theodore Cohn, a compensation expert, likes to talk about the Dutch company, Philips, in which twice-yearly bonuses can run up to 40% of base pay. "Managers say that a paper clip never hits the floor—a hand will be there to catch it," Cohn recounts. "If a husband dies, the wake is at night so that no one misses work. If someone goes on vacation, somebody else is shown how to do the job. There is practically no turnover."

Similarly, Cohn claims that at Lincoln Electric, where performance-related pay is twice the average factory wage, peer pressure can be so high that the first two years of employment are called purgatory.[4]

Another kind of pressure also emerges from equity-ownership and profit-sharing systems—the pressure to open the books, to disclose managerial salaries, and to justify pay differentials. Concerns like these bubble up when employees who may never have thought much about other people's pay suddenly realize that "their" money is at stake.

These concerns and questions of distributional equity are all part of making the system more fair as well as more effective. Perhaps the biggest issue, and the one most disturbing to traditionalists, is what happens to the chain of command when it does not match the progression of pay. If subordinates can outearn their bosses, hierarchy begins to crumble.

Social psychologists have shown that authority relationships depend on a degree of inequality. If the distance between boss and subordinate declines, so does automatic deference and respect. The key word here is *automatic*. Superiors can still gain re-

spect through their competence and fair treatment of subordinates. But power shifts as relationships become more equal.

Once the measures of good performance are both clearly established and clearly achieved, a subordinate no longer needs the goodwill of the boss quite so much. Proven achievement reflected in earnings higher than the boss's produces security, which produces risk taking, which produces speaking up and pushing back. As a result, the relationship between boss and subordinate changes from one based on authority to one based on mutual respect.

This change has positive implications for superiors as well as subordinates. For example, if a subordinate can earn more than the boss and still stay in place, then one of the incentives to compete for the boss's job is removed. Gone, too, is the tension that can build when an ambitious subordinate covets the boss's job and will do anything to get it. In short, if some of the *authority* of hierarchy is eliminated, so is some of the *hostility*.

In most traditional organizations, however, the idea of earning more than the boss seems insupportable and, to some people, clearly inequitable. There are, of course, organizational precedents for situations in which people in lower ranked jobs are paid more than those above. Field sales personnel paid on commission can often earn more than their managers; star scientists in R&D laboratories may earn more than the administrators nominally placed over them; and hourly workers can make more than their supervisors through overtime pay or union-negotiated wage settlements. But these situations are usually uncommon, or they're accepted because they're part of a dual-career ladder or the price of moving up in rank into management.

To get a feeling for the kinds of difficulties pay imbalances can create in hierarchical organizations, let's look at a less extreme case in which the gap between adjacent pay levels diminishes but does not disappear. This is called pay compression, and it bothers executives who believe in maintaining hierarchy.

In response to an American Management Association survey of 613 organizations, of which 134 were corporations with more than $1 billion in sales, 76% reported problems with compression.[5] Yet only a few percentage points divide the organizations expressing concern from those that do not. For example, the average earnings difference between first-line production supervisors and the highest paid production workers was 15.5% for organizations reporting com-

4 Theodore H. Cohn, "Incentive Compensation in Smaller Companies," *Proceedings of the Annual Conference of the American Compensation Association* (Scottsdale, Ariz.: ACA, 1984), pp. 1-7.

5 James W. Steele, *Paying for Performance and Position* (New York: AMA Membership Publishing Division, 1982).

pression problems, and only a little higher, 20%, for those not reporting such problems. In the maintenance area, the difference was even less – a 15.1% average earnings difference for those who said they had a problem versus 18.2% for those who said they did not. Furthermore, for a large number of companies claiming a compression problem, the difference between levels is actually greater than their official guidelines stipulate.

What is most striking to me, however, is how great the gap between adjacent levels still is – at least 15% difference in pay. Indeed, it is hard to avoid the conclusion that the executives concerned about compression are responding not to actual problems but to a perceived threat and the fear that hierarchy will crumble because of new pay practices.

What organizations say they will and won't do to solve compression problems supports this interpretation. While 67.4% of those concerned agree that an instant-bonus program would help, 70.1% say their companies would never institute one. And while 47.9% say that profit sharing for all salaried supervisors would help, 64.7% say that their companies would never do that either. In fact, the solutions least likely to be acceptable were precisely those that would change the hierarchy most – for example, reducing the number of job classifications, establishing fewer wage levels, and granting overtime compensation for supervisors (in effect, equalizing their status with that of hourly workers). On the other hand, the most favored solutions involved aids to upward mobility like training and rapid advancement that would keep the *structure* of the hierarchy intact while helping individuals move within it.

Innovative thoughts

The attacks on pay I've identified all push in the same direction. Indeed, they overlap and reinforce each other as, for example, a decision to reward individual contributors makes otherwise latent concerns about equity much more visible and live. Without options, private concerns can look like utopian dreams. Once those dreams begin to appear plausible, however, what was "the way things have to be" becomes instead a deliberate withholding of fair treatment.

By creating new forms for identifying, recognizing, and ultimately permitting contributions, the attack on pay goes beyond pay to color relationships throughout an organization. In the process, the iron cage of bureaucracy is being rattled in ways that will eventually change the nature, and the meaning, of hierarchy in ways we cannot yet imagine.

Wise executives, however, can prepare themselves and their companies for the revolutionary changes ahead. The shift toward contribution-based pay makes sense on grounds of equity, cost, productivity, and enterprise. And there are ways to manage that shift effectively. Here are some options to consider:

☐ Think strategically and systematically about the organizational implications of every change in compensation practices. If a venture unit offers an equity stake to participants, should a performance-based bonus with similar earning potential be offered to managers of mainstream businesses? If gain sharing is implemented on the shop floor, should it be extended to white-collar groups?

☐ Move toward reducing the fixed portion of pay and increasing the variable portion. Give business unit managers more discretion in distributing the variable pool, and make it a larger, more meaningful amount. Or allow more people to invest a portion of their salary in return for a greater share of the proceeds attributed to their own efforts later on.

☐ Manage the jealousy and conflict inherent in the more widely variable pay of nominal peers by making standards clear, giving everyone similar opportunities for growth in earnings, and reserving a portion of the earnings of stars or star sectors for distribution to others who have played a role in the success. Balance individual and group incentives in ways appropriate to the work unit and its tasks.

☐ Analyze – and, if necessary, rethink – the relationship between pay and value to the organization. Keep in mind that organizational levels defined for purposes of coordination do not necessarily reflect contributions to performance goals, and decouple pay from status or rank. And finally, be prepared to justify pay decisions in terms of clear contributions – and to offer these justifications more often, to more stakeholder groups. ▽

The beauty of most compensation plans is that
they always reward performance — however dismal it is.

Four Ways to Overpay Yourself Enough

by KENNETH MASON

The figures are out. Amid the blossoming of the spring's proxy statements came news of the annual salaries of the country's top executives. True, many people have found the numbers unconscionably high. Are they too high? Think of the pressure the CEO must withstand and the talent he or she must possess.

Maybe they're too low. But some companies have lost money under such well-paid helmsmanship.

How fortunate that we live in a scientific age. We don't have to ponder whether top executives are being compensated fairly. We can simply choose one of four approaches that have dominated executive remuneration planning for most of this century. Each school of thought, of course, has airtight logic and guarantees that shareholder value will be protected.

The Iron Law School. This school's central tenet is the Iron Law of Wages, according to which executives' compensation should be exactly equal to the amount that they require to subsist and reproduce, so as to perpetuate the executive population. Because of the remarkable biological diversity of executives, descended as they are from vastly different genetic pools, proponents of this theory have had to develop an enormous data base in its support. According to

Kenneth Mason is a former president of the Quaker Oats Company and a former director of Rohm and Haas and Harper & Row. He retired from Quaker Oats in 1979 and from all other business commitments in 1987. He now resides on the coast of Maine and is writing a novel about the inner workings of a large multinational food company.

the 1987 figures, in manufacturing concerns with $1 billion to $5 billion annual sales, entry-level accountants joining the controller's department require $24,000 per year to subsist. Beginning-level MBAs joining the marketing department require $37,500 to subsist.

Managers of Midwestern food plants employing approximately 1,000 workers can subsist on $80,000 per year plus a modest bonus, but New York advertising agency account executives supervising three peo-

 Too many executives get entrepreneurs' rewards for bureaucrats' jobs.

ple cannot. Just a few years ago, most *Fortune* "500" CEOs could feed and clothe themselves and their families on less than $1 million per year. Today, perhaps as a result of ozone depletion and acid rain, a rapidly increasing number need more.

The School of Supply and Demand. Followers of this school hold that executives' salaries are determined by the relationship between how many executives there are and how many are wanted. Lee Iacocca was happy to go to work for Chrysler at a salary of only $1 a year because he knew that while there was a vast supply of automobile executives clamoring for the job, there was demand for only one.

The forces of supply and demand also account for the enormous incomes earned by stockbrokers and

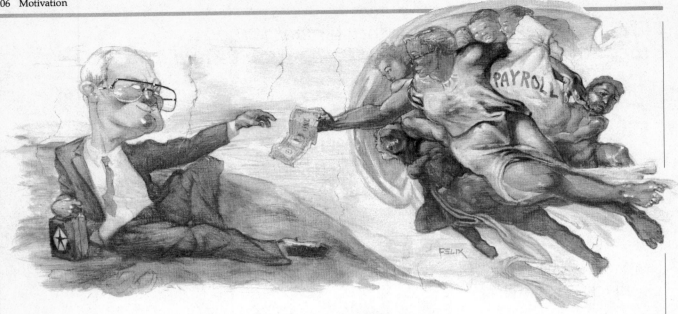

**With so many executives clamoring for the job,
Iacocca gladly accepted an annual salary of one dollar.**

investment bankers. Most Wall Street firms will not even interview a candidate who does not have a post-graduate degree in moral philosophy, and it is a Street rule that all new employees serve a five-year apprenticeship before being permitted to contact clients directly. In view of these rigorous educational and training requirements, it is hardly surprising that few young people are attracted to a career on Wall Street these days, and that those who are can command exceptionally high salaries.

The Hay Entitlement School. It was at Camp Maxey, Texas in 1941 that an obscure master sergeant solved the problem of getting 60,000 southern draftees to salute the one black officer on the post. He simply announced that in the military you salute the uniform, not the person.

This theory's most important postwar extrapolation is the Hay Entitlement System, which posits that there is a salary range for every job title, and you pay the job title, not the job holder. One attractive feature of the Hay system is that the salary ranges allow wide discretion in determining the wages actually to be paid the executive. If performance is clearly unsatisfactory, for instance, the incumbent's pay can be held within the high-middle and low-high part of the range.

The flexibility of the Hay system also has great appeal to management: the Hay team stands ready at all times to add points to any job title whose salary maximum is preventing an increase for an incumbent who doesn't merit promotion to a higher-rated

position but who is the kind of decent chap one hates to disappoint.

The Pay for Performance School. This school's highly controversial compensation theory originated in the world of professional sports. It first attracted general attention when Babe Ruth, on being asked how he could justify making more money than President Hoover, replied, "I had a better year than he did." Compensation theorists immediately recognized that the concept of linking compensation to such clear criteria as runs batted in or goals scored or sales quotas met or profit plans achieved had some real advantages over the compensation systems generally in use at that time.

The greatest advantage of the Pay for Performance approach is that, unlike the Iron Law theory, the Supply-Demand method, and the Hay Entitlement system, it enables the compensatee to play a role in the compensation process. It also allows participants to relate compensation not just to the past or present but also to the future—not just to the kind of job the executive used to do, not just to the kind of job the executive is doing now, but also to the kind of job you wish the executive would do.

This novel and powerful idea of compensation as incentive caused the emergence of a faction group, whose leaders have dominated Pay for Performance thinking throughout the post-Ruthian era. Their contributions to the discipline include such incentive devices as phantom stock, Stock Appreciation Rights, the Golden Handcuff, the Golden Parachute, and, most recently, the Golden Walking Stick and the Golden Rocking Chair.

The test of any managerial tool, compensation policy included, is its effectiveness in helping achieve management's operating goals. The goal most frequently proclaimed number one by America's 1,000 largest corporations in 1987 was to increase shareholder value. Do any of the four schools of compensation support that goal?

Does the Iron Law, a school whose central thesis derives from the discredited ideas of Malthus and whose followers ignore important contemporary shibboleths like quarterly earnings and P-E ratios? Obviously not. Which is not to say the Iron Law is totally without merit in regard to shareholder value. By ensuring that each executive is paid no more than what is needed to subsist and send one child through business school, the Iron Law curbs the lavish salaries, bonuses, pensions, and postretirement consulting contracts that have reduced the earnings and, by extension, the shareholder value of more than a few American corporations in recent years. Unfortunately, restraining executives' compensation, as opposed to controlling the conditions under which it is paid, has never been shown to improve shareholder value over the long term.

According to the School of Supply and Demand, strong demand for executives committed to increasing shareholder value will create a supply of those executives, and as these executives are hired, shareholder value will creep up. While this is a highly plausible theory, in real life things are different. The demand for executives committed to shareholder value does not create a supply of executives committed to shareholder value; it creates a supply of candidates committed to being interviewed for a high-paying job. While some of these candidates may indeed have the capability of increasing shareholder value, a correlation between use of the Law of Supply and Demand for compensation and a rise in shareholder value has never been established.

It is surprising, but unfortunately true, that the Hay Entitlement system, despite its modern genesis, also has proved unhelpful to corporations whose goal is to increase shareholder value. By rating jobs instead of executives, the Hay system produces a corporate environment in which managers compete with each other for the best jobs instead of the best results. With rare exceptions, shareholder value is an objective in name only when the Hay team has been at work. Although more than 90% of companies using the Hay system increased shareholder value significantly during the 1980s, they did so by virtue of policies and conditions unrelated to compensation.

Of all the approaches to executive compensation, one would expect Pay for Performance to be the best for boosting shareholder value. A plan that ties compensation to results surely must produce those results, at least over the long term. Yet in practice, Pay for Performance works no better than the other compensation theories. The problem is that management tends to introduce a new incentive plan the moment it appears that disappointing operating results are going to produce disappointing executive bonuses. When profits are rising, compensation is tied to profits. When they begin to sink, the plan switches. Suddenly compensation is tied to achieving a corporate ROI equal to industry ROI. If results fall short of industry ROI, the compensation plan is again revised to link pay to improving ROE by a point or two.

In the 1975-1983 period, the compensation incentive plans of the 200 largest industrial companies in the United States had an average life span of less than 18 months. The Pay for Performance school seems to have evolved into the KCR school, whose theory is Keep Compensation Rising no matter what.

A familiar example of KCR at work is the underwater stock option. What better executive incentive than the stock option for a corporation whose objective is to augment shareholder value? The executive doesn't benefit unless the shareholder does. No tickee, no washee, right? Wrong, says KCR. No tickee, we give you new tickee. Within days after 1987's Black Monday stock market crash, the business press was reporting that several major corporations planned to replace their executives' newly drowned options.

 When companies pay CEOs in stock, they should buy it at market rates.

This is exactly what many corporations did after the market decline of 1973. The experience of one high-level executive in the food industry is typical of that era. In 1973, he was granted an option for 2,500 shares of his corporation's stock at $40. Just after that, profits slumped. Two years later, the company replaced his stock option award with one for 7,000 shares at $15. He was not penalized by the company's decline in shareholder value; indeed, his financial future was actually enhanced as a result of it.

It's questionable whether stock options are effective incentives even in normal times because they seldom constitute a meaningful percentage of an executive's anticipated long-term compensation. True, options often turn out to be worth a lot, but for most executives they are just extra icing on an already well-frosted cake. A refreshing exception was Lee Iacocca's $1-a-year salary buttressed by a huge stock option award. His eventual payoff was enormous, but so was the risk of Chrysler going under, in which case he would have received very little.

It is a sad commentary on the intellectual vigor and financial discipline of the U.S. business community that so many corporate executives are receiving entrepreneurs' rewards for doing bureaucrats' jobs. The important decision-making jobs in American corporations today hardly ever entail financial risk to anyone except the shareholders. If my compensation package awards me $1.5 million when I meet the corporate profit plan and $1 million when I don't, where's my risk? Succeed or fail, the 20 top executives in most large corporations are almost certain to become wealthy.

Even getting fired is generally no financial blow to these executives. Personnel experts delight in figuring out a generous severance package for an executive who has been sacked after running a profitable division into the ground or making a fantastically dumb acquisition or launching five consecutive new product failures. They may not condone the executive's disastrous business decisions, but they will defend with their lives his or her right to be paid almost as much as if those decisions had been good ones. A typical severance package for an executive who has done a really bad job consists of a couple years' salary, a consulting contract, and a pension supplement giving the executive the same pension payments in early retirement that he would have gotten had he been sufficiently competent to stay the course. One executive's early retirement package included the merit increase he would have received at his annual review a few months hence had he not been fired for poor performance!

Executives' financial rewards must be linked more clearly and more emphatically to shareholders' if increasing shareholder value continues to be the first priority of U.S. corporations, and if compensation strategies are expected to play a role in achieving that objective. The Shareholder-Executive Linkage Formula (SHELF), a new incentive compensation strategy, tightens that link by introducing three long-overdue financial and ethical constraints into the corporate compensation process:

1. The annual cash compensation paid to executives of publicly held companies is limited to either 250% of the salary of the president of the United States or 25% of the compensation of the prior year's most valuable player in the National Basketball Association, whichever a corporation feels better fits its image. Are your executives more like President Reagan or Larry Bird? Strict observance of the limit by all publicly held corporations is enforced by the SEC.

2. Compensation in excess of the cash limit may be paid only in the publicly traded stock of the company. This stock must be purchased by the company on the open market and must be held by the executive for a minimum of five years. The company provides an annual interest-free loan to cover the annual income taxes due on this compensation. The executives repay the loans when they sell the shares or when they leave the company, whichever comes first.

3. The executive stock option is declared illegal and replaced by the Simultaneous Call and Put. A SCAP gives an executive a three-year call on one share of stock at a strike price of 130% of market

Why not limit executive pay to 25% of Larry Bird's salary?

price on the day of grant less dividends paid during the three-year period. At the same time, the executive commits to a three-year put on identical terms.

While some critics have dismissed SHELF as overly complicated, too risky, even radical, the plan is in no way at odds with the conventional compensation theories American industry is now following. The proposed presidential or Birdian limit on cash compensation, for instance, is entirely consistent with the Iron Law's subsistence requirement. Since the president of the United States pays no rent, it is not surprising that a CEO should require two-and-a-half times the president's wage to subsist and reproduce. Conversely, the sports star's shortened career span justifies his 4 to 1 advantage over CEOs, who often persuade their boards to let them keep playing into their dotage.

Nor does an upper limit on cash compensation violate the Law of Supply and Demand. There never has been a demand for high-salaried executives, only a large supply. The demand is for high-*performance* executives. Here there is also a large supply, but current compensation is not always a reliable clue to their identity. Many corporate executives now brazenly pay themselves annual salaries and bonuses that bear no correlation whatsoever to what any manager or company can accomplish in a single year. A corporation's paying $1 million a year for a run-of-the-mill CEO is not unlike the Pentagon's paying $150 for an ashtray: in both cases you know one just as good can be had for much less. The SEC has scores of regulations on its books designed to protect investors' interests in publicly held companies, yet under present regulations there is nothing to prevent a corporation from paying its CEO $1 million a week if it so decides. Shouldn't the shareholder be protected from such a move?

The requirement that all compensation over the cash limit be in the form of company stock and that this stock be purchased by the company on the open market serves a two-fold purpose. One is to make executives more appreciative of shareholder concerns by replacing no-risk stock options with normal-risk shares purchased at the price everyone else pays. The second is to provide a trickle-down benefit to the shareholders: the more executives are paid, the more stock the company must buy on the open market. This puts upward pressure on the stock price, boosting shareholder value.

Replacing stock options with SCAPs would put an end to a form of insider self-dealing that is extremely unfair to shareholders. Why should insiders be allowed to purchase shares at what is often a fraction of the price the public must pay? How is it fair to shareholders to dilute their ownership positions by issuing new shares for this purpose?

A call makes much more sense for executives and shareholders alike. Basing its strike price on a 10% annual growth premium makes it fair to the shareholder, while the automatic expiration date eliminates executive risk in timing the exercising of an option as well as any concern about trading on insider information. And pairing a company put with an executive call corrects a serious weakness of stock options as incentive compensation: options are a pleasant incentive when the stock is going up, but managers tend to lose interest when it isn't. With the call-put combination, managers never lose interest, no matter which direction the stock is going in.

How might a typical well-paid corporate executive expect to fare under SHELF? Consider the pretax compensation of a top executive in a large information systems company over a six-year period in the 1980s. Under a conventional compensation plan, her salary and bonus were $550,000 in year one,

$600,000 in year two, $750,000 when profits surged in year three, and $700,000 for each of years four, five, and six, when profits fell and then flattened. She also received an annual stock option grant equivalent to one-fifth of compensation. The option prices and quantities for years one through six are as follows:

3,667 shares at $30	2,000 shares at $70
1,600 shares at $75	2,154 shares at $65
1,500 shares at $100	2,333 shares at $60

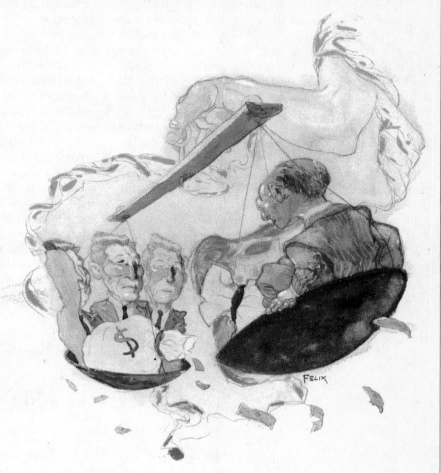

How many U.S. presidents is one executive worth?

Annual dividend payout during the period was $1.80, $2.00, $2.25, and, for each of the last three years, $2.50. For the whole six-year period, this executive received $4 million in cash compensation and had a paper profit of $110,000 in options for 3,667 shares of stock.

Now look at the pretax compensation history of the same executive under SHELF. Assuming the company had chosen the presidential cash cap, her cash compensation would have been $500,000 for each of the six years. Her compensation in excess of the cap would have been paid over the six years in the form of 14,766 shares of the company's stock with a current value of $885,960. In addition, the 3,667 call options received the first year would have to be exercised in year four. The strike price is calculated like this:

($30 stock price × 130%) −
($1.80 + $2.00 + $2.25) = $32.95

Since the market price of the stock in year four is $70, the executive makes a profit of:

($70 − $32.95) × 3,667 shares = $135,862

In year five, however, she has to pay the company $41,200 for the shareholders' year-two put and in year six, $93,750 for the year-three put. At $912, her call-put net for the period almost breaks even, making her total compensation for the period $3,886,872, 5% less than she would have received under the conventional method.

Now consider the future. The company's objective is to increase shareholder value. It did well at the beginning of the period, but shareholder value has declined for three straight years. Which executive has the stronger incentive to turn the company around? The executive under the conventional plan, who currently has a paper profit of $110,000 in her options and stands to make an additional paper profit of $268,710 if the stock gets back to $100 before the options expire? Or the executive under SHELF, who

owns 14,766 shares of the company's stock, the value of which will increase by $590,640 if the price goes back up to $100, who stands to make $151,366 on her current calls if the stock gets back to $100 next year, and who could lose $108,115 if the stock stays where it is for another three years?

Radical though it appears to some, the Shareholder-Executive Linkage Formula proposes only two quite modest refinements to present methods of executive compensation. The first requires compensation at the highest levels to be in the form of company stock. It affects only the handful of corporate executives who make the kinds of decisions the original owners of the business made before they took the company public. As owner surrogates, shouldn't these managers share some of the risks of ownership as well as the rewards? And mightn't this dramatically improve their decision making?

The second refinement replaces stock options with simultaneous calls and puts. The call portion of SCAPs corrects the basic unfairness to shareholders of selling stock to corporate insiders at lower than market prices. The put portion does something even more important: it prevents top corporate executives from walking away from a losing game for shareholders without losing something themselves.

Too radical? Too tough? Or high time.   ⎅

Reprint 88408

QUALITY vs. QUANTITY

INNING	1	2	3	4	5	6	7	8	9	TOTAL
QUALITY	0	1	0	0	2	0	0	1	0	4
QUANTITY	3	8	8	5	2	9	7	4	3	49

D. Fradon

Kevin J. Murphy

Top executives are worth every nickel they get

Each spring, critics, journalists, and special-interest groups devour hundreds of corporate proxy statements in a race to determine which executive gets the most for allegedly doing the least. They're running the wrong race.

> *"On average, compensation policies encourage executives to act on behalf of their shareholders and to put in the best managerial performance they can."*

The "excessive" compensation paid these greedy types, we are told, gouges the nation's 30 million shareholders. Their salaries are arbitrarily set at outrageous levels without regard to either profitability or performance. Moreover, the six- and seven-digit base salaries are just the tip of the compensation iceberg—executives fatten their already sizable paychecks severalfold through bonuses, stock options, and other short- and long-term incentive plans. As a result, the public view prevails that executives are paid too much for what they do and that compensation policies are irrational and ignore the needs of shareholders.

Mr. Murphy is an assistant professor at the Graduate School of Management of the University of Rochester, where he teaches economics. A recognized expert in the field of executive compensation, he consults with a wide range of corporations on their practices and has published in the Journal of Accounting and Economics *and, with Michael Jensen, in the* New York Times.

Simply put, the public view is wrong and based on fundamental misconceptions about the managerial labor market. One reason for these misconceptions is that executive compensation is an emotional issue. And because critics become wound up in their emotions, they rely on a blend of opinion, intuition, and carefully selected anecdotes to prove their points.[1] Of course, such anecdotal evidence is not useless and may even be valuable in identifying abuses in the compensation system when carefully interpreted. Critics cannot use such evidence, however, to show compensation trends or to support across-the-board condemnations of compensation policies.

I have devised a better way to test the validity of the complaints about executive pay by subjecting each proposition to a series of logical and statistical tests. My data are drawn, in part, from an examination of the compensation policies of almost 1,200 large U.S. corporations over ten years and are supplemented by the findings of a 1984 University of Rochester symposium, "Managerial Compensation and the Managerial Labor Market."[2] My results paint a very different picture of executive compensation by showing that:

☐   The pay and performance of top executives are strongly and positively related. Even without a direct link between pay and performance, executives' incomes are tied to their companies' performance through stock options, long-term performance plans, and, most important, stock ownership.

☐   Compensation proposals like short- and long-term incentive plans and golden parachutes actually benefit rather than harm shareholders.

☐   Changes in SEC reporting requirements and a shift toward compensation based on long-term performance explain most of the apparent compensation "explosion." This shift links compensation closely to shareholder wealth and motivates managers to look beyond next quarter's results.

| Exhibit I | **Relationship between rate of return on common stock and percentage changes in executive salary and bonus** 1975-1984 |

	1975-1984		1975-1979		1980-1984	
Annual rate of return on common stock	Number of executive-years in sample	Average annual change in salary and bonus	Number of executive-years in sample	Average annual change in salary and bonus	Number of executive-years in sample	Average annual change in salary and bonus
Entire sample	6,523	7.8 %	3,314	6.9 %	3,209	8.8 %
Less than −20 %	639	0.4 %	257	0.5 %	382	0.4 %
−20 % to 0 %	1,734	5.3 %	1,002	5.5 %	732	4.9 %
0 % to 20 %	1,917	8.3 %	989	7.5 %	928	9.2 %
20 % to 40 %	1,212	9.6 %	538	7.1 %	674	11.6 %
More than 40 %	1,021	13.8 %	528	11.1 %	493	16.6 %

Note:
Rates of return and percentage pay increases have been adjusted for inflation. As an example of how the rate of return is calculated, suppose that a share of stock worth $ 10 at the beginning of the year had increased in price to $ 12 by the end of the year and that the company paid cash dividends of $ 1 per share during the year. The holder of a share of the company's common stock would have realized a return of $ 3, or 30 % for the year. Salary and bonus data were constructed from *Forbes* annual compensation surveys from 1975 to 1984. The sample consists of 1,948 executives in 1,191 corporations.

Of course, some executives are overpaid or underpaid or paid in a way unrelated to performance. But, on average, I have found that compensation policies encourage executives to act on behalf of their shareholders and to put in the best managerial performance they can.

Pay & performance

Because shareholders are the owners of the corporation, it makes sense to analyze the executive compensation controversy from their perspective. One way to motivate managers is to structure compensation policies that reward them for taking actions that benefit their shareholders and punish them for taking actions that harm their shareholders. Shareholders measure corporations in terms of stock price and dividend performance. Thus a sensible compensation policy would push an executive's pay up with good price performance and down with poor performance.

A common criticism of compensation policies is that they encourage executives to focus on short-term profits rather than on long-term performance. Assuming efficient capital markets, current stock price reflects all available information about a company, thus making its stock market performance the appropriate measure of its long-term potential. My analysis (shown in *Exhibits I* and *II*) indicates that compensation gives executives the incentive to focus on the long term since it is implicitly or explicitly linked to their companies' stock market performance.

The statistics in *Exhibit I* compare the rate of return on common stock (including price appreciation and dividends) with percentage changes in top executives' salaries and bonuses over ten years. I have grouped the data, which represent sample averages, by the companies' stock price performance, but experiments with alternative measures like sales growth and return on equity yield similar qualitative results.

Throughout the ten-year period, executives received inflation-adjusted average annual increases in salary and bonus of 7.8%; more important is the positive relationship shown between the rate of return on common stock and average percentage changes in salary and bonus. When returns were less than −20%, executives received pay increases of only .4%; when performance exceeded 40%, pay increases averaged 13.8%.

As *Exhibit I* shows, the relationship between pay and performance has remained positive over time and has actually become stronger in recent years. Chief executives in companies with returns greater

Author's note: I am indebted to Michael Jensen and Jerold Zimmerman for their help. I gratefully acknowledge financial support from the Managerial Economics Research Center.

than 40% received inflation-adjusted average annual increases in salary and bonus of 11.1% from 1975 to 1979 and 16.6% from 1980 to 1984.

You can also use statistical regression techniques to estimate changes in executives' salaries and bonuses corresponding to each additional 10% of shareholder return. A company realizing a 10% return on its common stock will boost executive pay by some percentage, and you can use an estimate of the average pay increase to measure the magnitude of the relationship between pay and performance. By dividing the sample into subperiods, you can see if the relationship between pay and performance strengthens or weakens over time.

Exhibit II shows the results of the regression analysis. For every 10% rise in a company's stock price over the ten-year sample, the top executive's salary and bonus rose an average of 1.1%. Moreover, the relationship was stronger in the last half of the decade than in the first half. For each 10% shareholder return, annual salaries and bonuses increased by .8% from 1975 to 1979 and by 1.5% from 1980 to 1984.

As measured by the rate of return on common stock, a strong, positive statistical relationship exists between executive pay and company performance. These results are sharply at odds with recent studies that compare pay levels with measures of profitability and conclude that compensation is independent of performance.[3] The problem with such studies is that they look at the level of executive compensation across companies at a particular time instead of considering the extent to which compensation varies with companies' performance *over time*. This is an important distinction. Whether a company has well-paid —or low-paid—executives tells us nothing about the sensitivity of pay to performance.

To illustrate, consider two well-documented relationships—the positive relationship between company size and executive compensation and the negative one between company size and the average rate of return realized by shareholders.[4] From these it follows that a large company would have low rates of return and well-paid executives, while a small company would have high rates of return and low-paid executives. You'd conclude that pay and performance didn't correlate, and you'd be right if you took this kind of snapshot of the relationships. But if you took a moving picture—that is, looked at the results over time—you'd see that the pay of individual executives and the performance of their companies are strongly and positively related.

It is better to study how executive pay varies from year to year in a given company. *Exhibit I* and *Exhibit II* show that changes in executive pay mirror changes in shareholders' wealth. Two studies presented at the Rochester symposium corroborate this

result. The first was based on a sample of 461 executives in 72 manufacturing companies over 18 years; in it I examined salary, bonus, stock options, deferred compensation, total compensation, and stock ownership. It shows that executive compensation parallels corporate performance as measured by the rate of return on common stock.[5]

Another study of 249 executives from as many companies from 1978 to 1980 reaches the same conclusion. It found a strong, positive correlation between changes in executive compensation and stock-price performance (adjusted for marketwide price changes). Ranking companies on the basis of their stock-price performance, it suggests that those in the top 10% will raise their executives' compensation by an inflation-adjusted 5.5% and those in the bottom 10% will lower pay by 4%. In addition, the study finds that chief executives in the bottom 10% of the performance ranking are almost three times more likely to leave their companies than executives in the top 10%.[6]

The expanded compensation package

Suppose that I had not found a positive relationship between cash compensation and performance. Could I then conclude that executives do not act on behalf of their shareholders? The point is not moot; although I've shown a positive relationship between cash compensation and performance, I could easily find some companies where the relationship does not exist. So it is important to determine whether *total* compensation policies are doing the best job possible.

To do so requires that you look at more than just salary and bonus. Most studies in the financial press consider *only* salary and bonus and ignore potentially crucial variables like restricted stock, stock options, and long-term performance plans. In fact, these plans have become increasingly important. By their very nature, these plans tie executives' ultimate compensation directly to their companies' performance.

Executives' holdings of their companies' common stock constitute a large part of their wealth. The value of these stock holdings obviously goes up in good years and down in bad ones, quite independently of any relationship between performance and base pay. Suppose an executive with $4 million of stock sees the share price drop 25%. Because of his company's poor performance in the securities market, he has lost a million dollars—a loss that trivializes anything a board of directors might do to his base pay.

To assess the importance of inside stock ownership, I collected a 20-year time series of

| Exhibit II | **Average increase in executive salary and bonus corresponding to each additional 10 % rate of return on common stock**
1975-1984 |

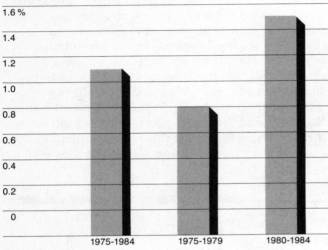

Estimated
percentage
change in
salary and
bonus

Note:
The percentage changes are estimated coefficients from regressions of percentage changes in salary and bonus on shareholder return. All estimates are statistically significant at confidence levels exceeding 99.99 %.

chief executive officer data from the proxy statements of 73 *Fortune* "500" manufacturing companies. Executives in this sample, which covered fiscal years 1964 through 1983, held an average (in 1984 constant dollars) of almost $7 million in their companies' common stock. Although this sample does not include shares held by family members and outside trusts, it does include a few executives with extraordinary stock holdings; the median stock holding for executives in this 20-year period is $1.5 million. That is, 50% of the chief executives in the 73 sample companies held more than $1.5 million in their companies' common stock.

Exhibit III depicts the relationships among company performance, salary and bonus, and changes in the value of executives' stock holdings for all chief executives in the 73 companies from 1964 to 1983. The point is clear; year-to-year changes in the value of executives' individual stock holdings often exceed their cash compensation. In companies with returns of less than −20%, executives lost an average of $2.9 million each on their stock holdings (compared with an average salary and bonus of $506,700); the median executive lost $643,800. In companies with returns greater than 40%, executives saw their stock

holdings go up by an average of $3.6 million each (the median figure was $635,600) compared with an average salary and bonus of $494,300.[7]

Does generosity backfire?

Executive employment contracts are determined by the board of directors, which in turn is elected by shareholders. A cooperative relationship between executives and their directors is usually required for corporate success, and some have incorrectly interpreted this fact as evidence that executives can set their own salaries by pushing their compensation plans past "captive" directors. A friendly relationship between executives and their boards does not mean that the executives are free of constraints; rather, constraints usually operate in subtle yet powerful ways.

For example, some corporations have adopted short- and long-term compensation plans that pay off only if the executives meet a certain performance standard. Golden parachutes, which compensate executives if they leave their company after a takeover, have also grown in popularity. If, as some critics contend, these plans benefit executives and harm shareholders, you would expect stock prices to fall at the announcement of the plan. Likewise, if these plans benefit shareholders, you would expect prices to rise.

Three symposium studies examined market reaction. One found that average stock prices rise by about 11% when companies make the first public announcement of bonus and other plans that reward short-term performance.[8] Another concluded that shareholders realize a 2% return when companies adopt long-term compensation plans.[9] A third study found that, on average, stock prices increase by 3% when companies announce the adoption of a golden parachute provision.[10] This favorable reaction supports the contention that golden parachutes benefit shareholders by removing managers' incentives to block economically efficient takeovers. The price increase may also indicate that takeovers are more likely when golden parachutes are adopted but does not indicate that these provisions harm shareholders.

In each study, stock values not only increase when companies announce compensation plans but also continue to trade at the new, higher levels. The studies thus support the idea that such plans help align the interests of executives and shareholders and signal "good times ahead" to the market. They refute the view that executives "overreach" when they adopt lucrative compensation schemes.

On average, executives do not harm shareholders when they alter employment-contract

Exhibit III	**Relationships among rate of return on common stock, executive salary and bonus, and change in value of inside stock holdings** 1964-1983				
Annual rate of return on common stock	**Number of executive-years in sample**	**Average annual salary and bonus**	**Average annual change in value of inside stock holdings**	**Median annual change in value of inside stock holdings**
Entire sample	1,394	$ 541,700	$ 270,900	$ 27,600
Less than −20 %	243	$ 506,700	−$ 2,914,200	−$ 643,800
−20 % to 0 %	361	$ 559,900	−$ 883,200	−$ 93,000
0 % to 20 %	360	$ 574,400	$ 560,600	$ 125,500
20 % to 40 %	223	$ 541,700	$ 2,260,700	$ 464,300
More than 40 %	207	$ 494,300	$ 3,594,500	$ 635,600

Note:
All variables have been adjusted for inflation (1984 constant dollars). Rate of return on common stock includes price appreciation and dividends. Inside stock holdings include only shares held directly and do not include shares held by family members or trusts. The change in the value of inside stock holdings is calculated by multiplying the value of each executive's share holdings (at the beginning of the fiscal year) by the rate of return on common stock. Data were constructed from proxy statements for 213 chief executives in 73 *Fortune* "500" manufacturing corporations from 1964 to 1983. Data were unavailable for 66 of the 1,460 possible executive-years.

provisions nor do they arbitrarily set their own salaries. If executives were truly able to set their salaries, why wouldn't they make them comparable with those of rock stars like Michael Jackson, whose income is many times that of even the highest paid executive? The only way the "set-their-own-salaries" argument works is if you assume that these salaries are somehow within some reasonable range of the competition—what other executives in similar industries are paid.

What's out of hand?

"Top management pay increases have gotten out of hand," warns Arch Patton, citing an apparent "explosion in top management compensation."[11] Indeed, a casual (but careless) look at compensation totals published in the business press seems to justify such concern. *Exhibit IV* shows the total compensation received by the nation's best paid executives from 1974 to 1984 using *Forbes* data (unadjusted for inflation). Before 1977, the fattest paycheck hovered around $1 million but then jumped to $3.4 million in 1978, $5.2 million in 1979, and $7.9 million in 1980. Warner Communications' Steven Ross shattered the eight-digit barrier with a total compensation of $22.6 million in 1981; in 1982, Frederick Smith of Federal Express received a total package of $51.5 million. The figure "plummeted" in 1983 to the mere $13.2 million received by NCR's retiring William Anderson but rebounded in 1984 to the $23 million received by Mesa's T. Boone Pickens, Jr.

A closer look at the data reveals that the apparent increase stems, in part, from a shift in the structure of compensation and has been exaggerated by changes in SEC reporting requirements. Moreover, the increase does not indicate that the conflict of interest between executives and their shareholders has worsened. Rather, the trend reflects a growing reliance on stock options and other long-term performance plans designed to link compensation more closely with shareholder wealth. The often spectacular payoffs are a once-in-a-lifetime experience.

For example, Frederick Smith's 1982 salary and bonus of $413,600 accounted for less than 1% of his $51.5 million total compensation; if the ranking had been based on salary and bonus alone, he wouldn't have made the top 300. NCR's William Anderson received only 8% of his 1983 compensation in the form of salary and bonus; his salary and bonus of $1,075,000 was only the nation's thirty-seventh highest. (Mr. Pickens's 1984 salary and bonus of $4.2 million was indeed the nation's highest but included $3 million for services provided in 1982 and 1983 when bonuses were not awarded.) In any given year, only a small percentage of executives enjoy big gains from stock options or other performance plans. The overwhelming majority get most of their compensation in the form of salaries and cash bonuses.

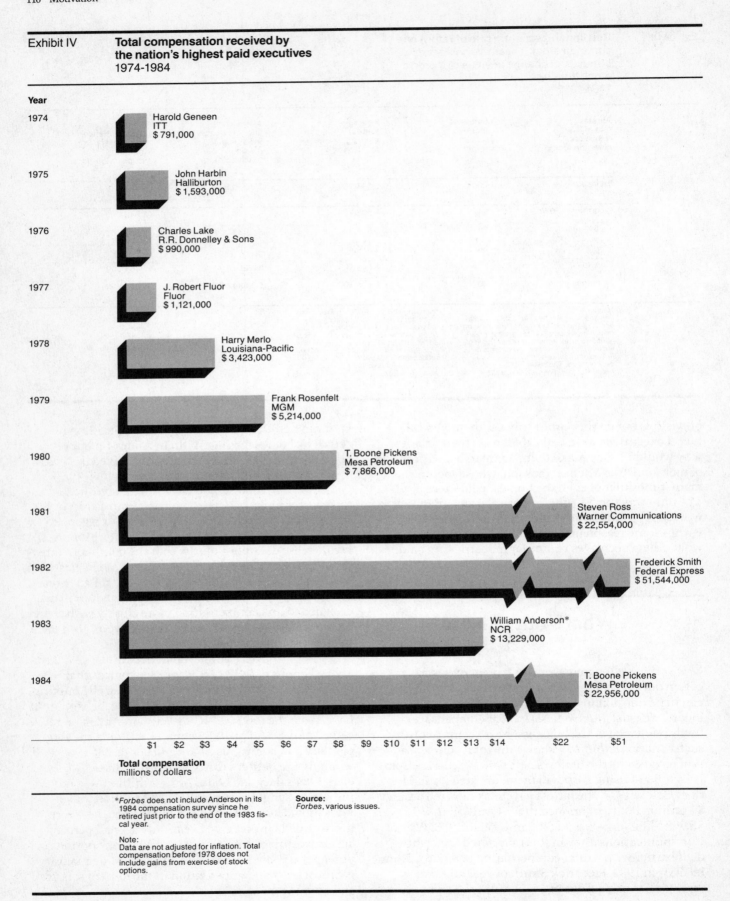

Exhibit IV

**Total compensation received by
the nation's highest paid executives
1974-1984**

Year

1974   Harold Geneen
        ITT
        $ 791,000

1975   John Harbin
        Halliburton
        $ 1,593,000

1976   Charles Lake
        R.R. Donnelley & Sons
        $ 990,000

1977   J. Robert Fluor
        Fluor
        $ 1,121,000

1978   Harry Merlo
        Louisiana-Pacific
        $ 3,423,000

1979   Frank Rosenfelt
        MGM
        $ 5,214,000

1980   T. Boone Pickens
        Mesa Petroleum
        $ 7,866,000

1981   Steven Ross
        Warner Communications
        $ 22,554,000

1982   Frederick Smith
        Federal Express
        $ 51,544,000

1983   William Anderson*
        NCR
        $ 13,229,000

1984   T. Boone Pickens
        Mesa Petroleum
        $ 22,956,000

$1 $2 $3 $4 $5 $6 $7 $8 $9 $10 $11 $12 $13 $14 $22 $51

Total compensation
millions of dollars

Forbes does not include Anderson in its
1984 compensation survey since he
retired just prior to the end of the 1983 fiscal year.

Source:
Forbes, various issues.

Note:
Data are not adjusted for inflation. Total
compensation before 1978 does not
include gains from exercise of stock
options.

Even so, the great popularity of stock options and other long-term performance plans has several implications. First, an executive's pay in any given year reflects amounts actually accrued or earned over several years and tends to increase the maximum compensation observed, just as a switch from weekly to monthly pay periods will increase the maximum compensation observed in any given week (for example, the last week of the month).

Second, long-term performance plans give high rewards for excellent performance but are neutral toward poor or mediocre performance. It's the same as designing a state lottery with one grand prize of $1 million rather than a hundred prizes of $10,000 each; you increase the amount paid to the winner but not the total amount awarded. If the chief executives of ten different companies were each awarded stock options at the beginning of the year, their value at the date of grant might be similar. By the end of the option period, however, only a few would be worth a great deal of money; the others would be worthless.

Third, most long-term performance plans are based on stock prices. The stock market boom produced high payoffs from 1981 to 1983, while the market decline in the 1970s produced low or zero payoffs. Thus an executive awarded an equal number of stock options or performance plan units each year would have realized zero gains during the stock market decline and large gains during the boom; cyclical movements produced increases in the dollar amounts realized even though the amounts granted under these plans remained relatively constant.

Finally, before 1978, the payoffs from stock options and other long-term plans were reported in a somewhat incomprehensible table at the back of corporate proxy statements. Changes in SEC reporting rules have moved these payoffs to the front of the statement, where they are much more accessible to the media. Compensation totals published in *Forbes* (see *Exhibit IV*) and other business periodicals before 1978 exclude option realizations; data published after 1978 include them. The editors of these compensation surveys warn against making year-to-year comparisons when the definitions have changed. Unfortunately, critics have often ignored these warnings.

Why such controversy?

The recent attacks on executive compensation come mainly from a few individuals and special-interest groups who use the controversy to further their own agendas. In 1984, for example, former U.S. Trade Representative William Brock assailed "excessive" auto executive bonuses to argue against Japanese import quotas. Labor unions have used the executive pay issue to bolster demands for higher wages for their members. Mark Green's condemnation of "overreaching" executives continues the general Nader-Green attack on the corporation. In each case, the executive compensation question is virtually unrelated to the ultimate objectives of the attackers.

Such highly publicized assaults cause confusion about executive compensation, a confusion exacerbated by the second-rate research conducted and reported by most media commentators. How compensation is determined is complex; current performance is only one of the many factors that affect executive pay. Thus performance cannot explain all or even most of an individual's compensation even though the relationship between pay and performance is strong, positive, and statistically significant. In any case, estimating the relationship between pay and performance is tricky and cannot be done by making simple cross-sectional comparisons.

Another source of confusion is the use of isolated examples and anecdotal evidence. The quoted numbers are usually taken out of context and fail to tell the whole story. Single examples purporting to show no relationship between pay and performance mislead since they often include big long-term payoffs but never changes in the value of the executive's stock holdings.

Some executives are undoubtedly abusing the compensation system, and anecdotal evidence may help identify and eliminate these excesses. I believe, however, that the true excesses are not made by the million-dollar executives, who are, by and large, rewarded for a history of superior performance in behalf of shareholders. Real abuses are more likely found among lower paid executives whose pay is both unrelated to performance and out of line with the pay of their peers in similar companies. Even if the critics were to identify real excesses, it is unfortunate that their isolated examples would help justify a blanket condemnation.

The nation's shareholders need not fear that they are being swindled by greedy executives. Compensation policies normally make a great deal of sense. Companies are, moreover, adopting compensation plans that benefit shareholders by creating better managerial incentives.

My evidence cannot prove that all or even most boards of directors are doing the best possible job of tying executive pay to company performance. Some executives are undoubtedly being overpaid, while others are being underpaid or paid in a way unrelated to performance. But even so, the evidence does indicate that executive compensation in U.S. corporations is characterized not by madness but by basic corporate common sense.

References

1 See, for example, Joseph E. Muckley, "'Dear Fellow Shareowner'," HBR March-April 1984, p. 46; Mark Green and Bonnie Tenneriello, "From Pay to Perks to Parachutes: The Trouble with Executive Compensation," Democracy Project Report No. 8, March 1984.

2 Papers presented at the symposium are published in the Journal of Accounting and Economics, April 1985.

3 See, for example, Carol Loomis, "The Madness of Executive Compensation," Fortune, July 1982, p. 42.

4 The relationship between compensation and sales is reported by Harland Fox, Top Executive Compensation, Report No. 854 (New York: Conference Board, 1985). Evidence relating company size and shareholder return appears in the Symposium on Size and Stock Returns, published in the Journal of Financial Economics, June 1983.

5 Kevin J. Murphy, "Corporate Performance and Managerial Remuneration: An Empirical Analysis," Journal of Accounting and Economics, April 1985, p. 11.

6 Anne T. Coughlan and Ronald M. Schmidt, "Executive Compensation, Management Turnover, and Firm Performance: An Empirical Investigation," Journal of Accounting and Economics, April 1985, p. 43.

7 For more evidence on the importance of executive stock holdings, see George J. Benston, "The Self-Serving Management Hypothesis: Some Evidence," Journal of Accounting and Economics, April 1985, p. 67.

8 Hassan Tehranian and James Waegelein, "Market Reaction to Short-Term Executive Compensation Plan Adoption," Journal of Accounting and Economics, April 1985, p. 131.

9 James Brickley, Sanjai Bhagat, and Ronald C. Lease, "The Impact of Long-Range Managerial Compensation Plans on Shareholder Wealth," Journal of Accounting and Economics, April 1985, p. 113.

10 Richard A. Lambert and David F. Larcker, "Golden Parachutes, Executive Decision Making, and Shareholder Wealth," Journal of Accounting and Economics, April 1985, p. 179.

11 Arch Patton, "Those Million-Dollar-A-Year Executives," HBR January-February 1985, p. 56.

The money-making citizen

By one class of journals, wealth, the science of wealth, and the classes that acquire wealth, are favorite topics of railing. The money-getting spirit is continually anathematized by all the believers in medieval virtue and patriarchal simplicity. They use the utmost license of vituperation, too, against the plodding industry of the mercantile and manufacturing classes; though no persons are more anxious than the literary hangers-on of the aristocracy, to rival or to share the wealth and the splendor of successful men of business. Our sentimental feudalists are never tired of writing against the grasping, hard-hearted money makers, and sowing dissension between them and the laborers. On this specific account, as well as illustrating a general principle of society, it is important to connect the peace of society with the progress of wealth.

In fact, every man who acquires anything by his industry gives by that a hostage to order. He becomes interested in possessing tranquillity in proportion to his acquisition. His savings are generally put out to interest. He relies therefore on the future. He depends on production hereafter. He is a creditor of society, and his advances can only be repaid by peace and success. Theoretically, the matter is perfectly plain. Those who are destitute must be ready for every change. Those who are industrious, provident, and wealthy are desirous of peace and enjoyment. But what is true of individuals seems, by writers against wealth, to be considered as not true of society, and the men who are assiduous in their respective callings, who look closely after their ledgers, and endeavor to win much and waste nothing, are satirized and vilified as publicly injurious. It is supposed, according to the old antitrade, antisocial theory, and according to some practices, too much honored by these writers, that all which the plodding classes gain, produce, or possess, is taken from somebody else. They have no faith in honest exertions, and seem to believe that they are not naturally rewarded. The bookseller who employs his capital in printing a work, which, but for his aid, would never be published at all, is accused of growing rich at the expense of authors. The manufacturer who erects a mill, and finds employment for a thousand persons, is too often described as injuring and oppressing those, who but for his inventions and schemes might have wanted food. It seems of some consequence to rescue the money-getting, wealth-making classes from this kind of undeserved opprobrium, by pointing out the connection between order and tranquillity...

From
"The Progress of Wealth and the Preservation of Order,"
The Economist,
July 14, 1849.

GROWING CONCERNS

How to conserve cash and still attract the best executives

Compensation and Benefits for Startup Companies

by Joseph S. Tibbetts, Jr. and
Edmund T. Donovan

You've decided to start a company. Your business plan is based on sound strategy and thorough market research. Your background and training have prepared you for the challenge. Now you must assemble the quality management team that venture investors demand. So you begin the search for a topflight engineer to head product development and a seasoned manager to handle marketing, sales, and distribution.

Attracting these executives is easier said than done. You've networked your way to just the marketing candidate you need: a vice president with the right industry experience and an aggressive business outlook. But she makes $100,000 a year in a secure job at a large company. You can't possibly commit that much cash, even if you do raise outside capital. How do you structure a compensation package that will lure her away? How much cash is reasonable? How much and what type of stock should the package include? Is there any way to match the ar-

ray of benefits—retirement plans, child-care assistance, savings programs—her current employer provides? In short, what kind of compensation and benefits program will attract, motivate, and retain this marketing vice president and other

> **Be realistic about your limitations. But don't ignore the advantages of being small.**

key executives while not jeopardizing the fragile finances of your startup business?

Selecting appropriate compensation and benefits policies is a critical challenge for companies of all sizes. But never are the challenges more difficult—or the stakes higher—than when a company first takes shape. Startups must strike a delicate balance. Unrealistically low levels of

cash compensation weaken their ability to attract quality managers. Unrealistically high levels of cash compensation can turn off potential investors and, in extreme cases, threaten the solvency of the business. How to proceed?

First, be realistic about the limitations. There is simply no way that a company just developing a prototype or shipping product for less than a year or generating its first black ink after several money-losing years of building the business can match the current salaries and benefits offered by established competitors. At the same time, there are real advantages to being small. Without an entrenched personnel bureaucracy and long-standing compensation policies, it is easier to tailor salaries and benefits to individual needs. Creativity and flexibility are at a premium.

Second, be thorough and systematic about analyzing the options. Compensation and benefits plans can be expensive to design, install, administer, and terminate. A program that is inappropriate or badly conceived can be a very costly mistake. Startups should evaluate compensation and benefits alternatives from four distinct perspectives.

How do they affect cash flow? Survival is the first order of business for a new company. Even if you have raised an initial round of equity financing, there is seldom enough working capital to go around. Research and development, facilities and equipment, and marketing costs all make priority claims on resources. Cash compensation must be a lower priority. Despite this awkward tension (the desperate need to attract first-rate talent without having the cash to pay them market rates), marshaling resources for pressing business needs must remain paramount.

What are the tax implications? Compensation and benefits choices

Joseph S. Tibbetts, Jr. is managing partner of the Price Waterhouse Entrepreneurial Services Center in Cambridge, Massachusetts. Edmund T. Donovan, a tax attorney, is manager of employee benefits services at Price Waterhouse in Boston.

have major tax consequences for a startup company and its executives; startups can use the tax code to maximum advantage in compensation decisions. Certain approaches, like setting aside assets to secure deferred compensation liabilities, require that executives declare the income immediately and the company deduct it as a current expense. Other

> No startup is an island. Factor regional and industry trends into your salary calculations.

approaches, like leaving deferred compensation liabilities unsecured, allow executives to declare the income later while the company takes a future deduction. Many executives value the option of deferring taxable income more than the security of immediate cash. And since most startups have few, if any, profits to shield from taxes, deferring deductions may appeal to them as well.

What is the accounting impact? Most companies on their way to an initial public offering or a sellout to a larger company must register particular earning patterns. Different compensation programs affect the income statement in very different ways. One service company in the startup stage adopted an insurance-backed salary plan for its key executives. The plan bolstered the company's short-term cash flow by deferring salary payments (it also deferred taxable income for those executives). But it would have meant heavy charges to book earnings over the deferral period— charges that might have interfered with the company's plans to go public. So management backed out of the program at the eleventh hour.

What is the competition doing? No startup is an island, especially when vying for talented executives. Companies must factor regional and industry trends into their compensation and benefits calculations. One

newly established law firm decided not to offer new associates a 401(k) plan. (This program allows employees to contribute pretax dollars into a savings fund that also grows tax-free. Many employers match a portion of their employees' contributions.) The firm quickly discovered that it could not attract top candidates without the plan; it had become a staple of the profession in that geographic market. So it established a 401(k) and assumed the administrative costs, but it saved money by not including a matching provision right away.

Events at a Boston software company illustrate the potential for flexibility in startup compensation. The company's three founders had worked together at a previous employer. They had sufficient personal resources to contribute assets and cash to the new company in exchange for founders' stock. They decided to forgo cash compensation altogether for the first year.

Critical to the company's success were five software engineers who would write code for the first product. It did not make sense for the company to raise venture capital to pay the engineers their market-value salaries. Yet their talents were essential if the company were to deliver the software on time.

The obvious solution: supplement cash compensation with stock. But two problems arose. The five prospects had unreasonably high expectations about how much stock they should receive. Each demanded 5% to 10% of the company, which, if granted, would have meant transferring excessive ownership to them. Moreover, while they were equal in experience and ability and therefore worth equal salaries, each had different cash requirements to meet their obligations and maintain a reasonable life-style. One of the engineers was single and had few debts; he was happy to go cash-poor and bank on the company's growth. One of his colleagues, however, had a wife and young child at home and needed the security of a sizable paycheck.

The founders devised a solution to meet the needs of the company and

its prospective employees. They consulted other software startups and documented that second-tier employees typically received 1% to 3% ownership stakes. After some negotiation, they settled on a maximum of 2% for each of the five engineers. Then they agreed on a formula by which these employees could trade cash for stock during their first three years. For every $1,000 in cash an engineer received over a base figure, he or she forfeited a fixed number of shares. The result: all five engineers signed on, the company stayed within its cash constraints, and the founders gave up a more appropriate 7% of the company's equity.

Cash vs. stock

Equity is the great compensation equalizer in startup companies—the bridge between an executive's market value and the company's cash constraints. And there are endless variations on the equity theme: restricted shares, incentive stock options, nonqualified options, stock appreciation rights (SARs), phantom stock, and the list goes on. This dizzying array of choices notwithstanding, startup companies face three basic questions. Does it make sense to grant key executives an equity interest? If so, should the company use restricted stock, options, or some combination of both? If not, does it make sense to reward executives based on the company's appreciating share value or to devise formulas based on different criteria?

Let's consider these questions one at a time. Some company founders are unwilling to part with much ownership at inception. And with good reason. Venture capitalists or other outside investors will demand a healthy share of equity in return for a capital infusion. Founders rightly worry about diluting their control before obtaining venture funds.

Alternatives in this situation include SARs and phantom shares— programs that allow key employees to benefit from the company's increasing value without transferring voting power to them. No shares actually trade hands; the company compensates its executives to reflect the appreciation of its stock. Many

"Peterson, run down and tell my wife that I'll come out and play as soon as I've wrapped up these contracts and not a minute before."

executives prefer these programs to outright equity ownership because they don't have to invest their own money. They receive the financial benefits of owning stock without the risk of buying shares. In return, of course, they forfeit the rights and privileges of ownership. These programs can get complicated, however, and they require thorough accounting reviews. Reporting rules for artificial stock plans are very restrictive and sometimes create substantial charges against earnings.

Some founders take the other extreme. In the interest of saving cash, they award bits of equity at every turn. This can create real problems. When it comes to issuing stock, startups should always be careful not to sell the store before they fill the shelves. That is, they should award shares to key executives and second-tier employees in a way that protects the long-term company interest. And these awards should

take place only after the company has fully distributed stock to the founders.

The choice of whether to issue actual or phantom shares should also be consistent with the company's strategy. If the goal is to realize the "big payoff" within three to five years through an initial public offering or outright sale of the company, then stock may be the best route. You can motivate employees to work hard and build the company's value since they can readily envision big personal rewards down the road.

The founder of a temporary employment agency used this approach to attract and motivate key executives. He planned from the start to sell the business once it reached critical mass, and let his key executives know his game plan. He also allowed them to buy shares at a discount. When he sold the business a few years later for $10 million, certain executives, each of whom had been

allowed to buy up to 4% of the company, received as much as $400,000. The lure of cashing out quickly was a great motivator for this company's top executives.

For companies that plan to grow more slowly over the first three to five years, resist acquisition offers, and maintain private ownership, the stock alternative may not be optimal. Granting shares in a company that may never be sold or publicly traded is a bit like giving away play money. Worthless paper can actually be a demotivator for employees.

In such cases, it may make sense to create an artificial market for stock. Companies can choose among various book-value plans, under which they offer to buy back shares issued to employees according to a pricing formula. Such plans establish a measurement mechanism based on company performance—like book value, earnings, return on assets or equity—that determines the company's per-share value. As with phantom shares and SARs, book-value plans require a thorough accounting review.

If a company does decide to issue shares, the next question is how to do it. Restricted stock is one alternative. Restricted shares most often require that an executive remain with the company for a specified time period or forfeit the equity, thus creating "golden handcuffs" to promote long-term service. The executive otherwise enjoys all the rights of other shareholders, except for the

> **Shares in a company that will never go public can actually demotivate your people.**

right to sell any stock still subject to restriction.

Stock options are another choice, and they generally come in two forms: incentive stock options (ISOs) and nonqualified stock options (NSOs). As with restricted shares, stock options can create golden handcuffs. Most options, whether ISOs or NSOs, involve a vesting schedule. Executives may receive options on 1,000 shares of stock, but only 25% of the options vest (i.e., executives can exercise them) in any one year. If an executive leaves the company, he or she loses the unexercised options. Startups often prefer ISOs since they give executives a timing advantage with respect to taxes. Executives pay no taxes on any capital gains until they sell or exchange the stock, and then only if they realize a profit over the exercise price. ISOs, however, give the company no tax deductions—which is not a major drawback for startups that don't expect to earn big profits for several years. Of course, if companies generate taxable income before their executives exercise their options, lack of a deduction is a definite negative.

ISOs have other drawbacks. Tax laws impose stiff technical requirements on how much stock can be subject to options, the maximum exercise period, who can receive options, and how long stock must be held before it can be sold. Moreover, the exercise price of an ISO cannot be lower than the fair market value of the stock on the date the option is granted. (Shares need not be publicly traded for them to have a fair market value. Private companies estimate the market value of their stock.)

For these and other reasons, companies usually issue NSOs as well as ISOs. NSOs can be issued at a discount to current market value. They can be issued to directors and consultants (who cannot receive ISOs) as well as to company employees. And they have different tax consequences for the issuing company, which can deduct the spread between the exercise price and the market price of the shares when the options are exercised.

NSOs can also play a role in deferred compensation programs. More and more startups are following the lead of larger companies by allowing executives to defer cash compensation with stock options. They grant NSOs at a below-market exercise price that reflects the amount of salary deferred. Unlike standard deferral plans, where cash is paid out on some unalterable future date (thus triggering automatic tax liabilities), the option approach gives executives control over when and how they will be taxed on their deferred salary. The company, meanwhile, can deduct the spread when its executives exercise their options.

One small but growing high-tech company used a combination of stock techniques to achieve several compensation goals simultaneously. It issued NSOs with an exercise price equal to fair market value (most NSOs are issued at a discount). All the options were exercisable immediately (most options have a vesting schedule). Finally, the company placed restrictions on the resale of stock purchased with options.

This program allowed for maximum flexibility. Executives with excess cash could exercise all their options right away; executives with less cash, or who wanted to wait for signs of the company's progress, could wait months or years to exercise. The plan provided the company with tax deductions on any options exercised in the future (assuming the fair market value at exercise exceeded the stock's fair market value when the company granted the options) and avoided any charges to book earnings in the process. And the resale restrictions created golden handcuffs without forcing executives to wait to buy their shares.

The benefits challenge

No startup can match the cradle-to-grave benefits offered by employers like IBM or General Motors, although young companies may have to attract executives from these giant companies. It is also true, however, that the executives most attracted to startup opportunities may be people for whom standard benefit packages are relatively unimportant. Startup companies have special opportunities for creativity and customization with employee benefits. The goal should not be to come as close to what IBM offers without going broke, but to devise low-cost, innovative programs that meet the needs of a small employee corps.

Of course, certain basic needs must be met. Group life insurance is important, although coverage levels should start small and increase as the company gets stronger. Group medical is also essential, although there are many ways to limit its cost. Setting higher-than-average deductibles lowers employer premiums (the deductibles can be adjusted downward as financial stability improves). Self-insuring smaller claims also conserves cash. One young com-

You'll never match IBM's benefits. So you have to be creative.

pany saved 25% on its health-insurance premiums by self-insuring the first $500 of each claim and paying a third party to administer the coverage.

The list of traditional employee benefits doesn't have to stop here—but it probably should. Most companies should not adopt long-term disability coverage, dental plans, child-care assistance, even retirement plans, until they are well beyond the startup phase. This is a difficult reality for many founders to accept, especially those who have broken from larger companies with generous benefit programs. But any program has costs—and costs of any kind are a critical worry for a new company trying to move from the red into the black. Indeed, one startup in the business of developing and operating progressive child-care centers wisely decided to wait for greater financial stability before offering its own employees child-care benefits.

Many young companies underestimate the money and time it takes just to administer benefit programs, let alone fund them. Employee benefits do not run on automatic pilot. While the vice president of marketing watches marketing, the CFO keeps tabs on finances, and the CEO snuffs out the fires that always threaten to engulf a young company, who is left to mind the personnel store? If a substantial benefits program is in place, someone has to handle the day-to-day administrative details and update the program as the accounting and tax rules change. The best strategy is to keep benefits modest at first and make them more comprehensive as the company moves toward profitability.

Which is not to suggest that the only answer to benefits is setting strict limits. Other creative policies may not only cost less but they also may better suit the interests and needs of executive recruits. Take company-supplied lunches. One startup computer company thought it was important to create a "think-tank" atmosphere. So it set up writing boards in the cafeteria, provided all employees with daily lunches from various ethnic restaurants, and encouraged spirited noontime discussions.

Certainly, Thai food is no substitute for a generous pension. But benefits that promote a creative and energetic office environment may matter more to employees than savings plans whose impact may not be felt for decades. One startup learned this lesson after it polled its employees. It was prepared to offer an attractive—and costly—401(k) program until a survey disclosed that employees preferred a much different benefit: employer-paid membership at a local health club. The company gladly obliged.

Deciding on compensation policies for startup companies means making tough choices. There is an inevitable temptation, as a company shows its first signs of growth and financial stability, to enlarge salaries and benefits toward market levels. You should resist these temptations. As your company heads toward maturity, so can your compensation and benefits programs. But the wisest approach is to go slowly, to make enhancements incrementally, and to be aware at all times of the cash flow, taxation, and accounting implications of the choices you face.

Reprint 89111

SPECIAL COLLECTIONS • BOOKS • HBR ARTICLES • CUSTOM HBR ARTICLES • VIDEOS • CASES

READ THE FINE PRINT

REPRINTS
Telephone: 617-495-6192
Fax: 617-495-6985

Current and past articles are available, as is an annually updated index. Discounts apply to large-quantity purchases.

Please send orders to HBR Reprints, Harvard Business School Publishing Division, Boston, MA 02163.

HOW CAN HARVARD BUSINESS REVIEW ARTICLES WORK FOR YOU?

For years, we've printed a microscopically small notice on the editorial credits page of the Harvard Business Review alerting our readers to the availability of HBR articles.

Now we invite you to take a closer look at how you can put this hard-working business tool to work for you.

IN THE CORPORATE CLASSROOM

There's no more effective, or cost-effective, way to supplement your corporate training programs than in-depth, incisive HBR articles.

At just $3.50 a copy—even less for quantity orders—it's no wonder hundreds of companies use HBR articles for management training.

IN-BOX INNOVATION

Where do your company's movers and shakers get their big ideas? Many find inspiration in the pages of HBR. They then share the wealth by distributing HBR articles to colleagues.

IN MARKETING AND SALES SUPPORT

HBR articles are a substantive leave-behind to your sales calls. They add credibility to your direct mail campaigns. And demonstrate that your company is on the leading edge of business thinking.

CREATE CUSTOM ARTICLES

If you want even greater impact, personalize HBR articles with your company's name or logo. And put your name in front of your customers.

DISCOVER MORE REASONS IN THE HBR CATALOG.

In all, the Harvard Business Review Catalog lists articles on over 500 different subjects. Plus, you'll find collections, books, and videos on subjects you need to know. The catalog is yours for just $10.00. Order today. And start putting HBR articles to work for you.

How To Order. To order individual articles or the HBR Catalog, dial toll-free in the continental U.S. 1-800-545-7685. Outside the U.S. call 617-495-6192. **Please mention telephone code 165A** when placing your order. Or FAX your order to 617-495-6985. You may also send a check payable to Harvard Business School Publishing Division, or credit card information to: HBR Articles, Harvard Business School Publishing Division, Operations Department, Boston, MA 02163. **All orders must be prepaid.**

Order No.	Title	Qty. X	Price +	Shipping =	Total
21018	Catalog		$10		

U.S. and Canada: 5% for UPS or first class mail. Foreign Surface Mail: 15% for parcel post registered; allow 3–6 mos. Express Deliveries (credit card orders only): billed at cost; all foreign orders not designating express delivery will be sent by registered surface mail.

☐ Check enclosed (in U.S. funds drawn on U.S. bank)

☐ VISA   ☐ American Express   ☐ MasterCard

Card Number _____ Exp. Date _____

Signature _____

Telephone _____ FAX _____

Name _____

Organization _____

Street _____

City _____

State/Zip _____

Country _____

Harvard Business School Publishing

☐ Home address   ☐ Organization address

PLEASE REFERENCE TELEPHONE ORDER SOURCE CODE 165A

SPECIAL COLLECTIONS • BOOKS • HBR ARTICLES • CUSTOM HBR ARTICLES • VIDEOS • CASES

YOU SAID: AND WE SAID:

❝Give us training tools that are relevant to our business...ones we can use *now*.❞

❝We need new cases that stimulate meaningful discussion.❞

❝It can't be a catalog of canned programs... everything we do is custom.❞

❝Make it a single source for up-to-date materials ...on the most current business topics.❞

❝Better yet if it's from a reputable business school. That adds credibility.❞

❝Introducing the Harvard Business School Corporate Training and Development Catalog.❞

You asked for it. And now it's here.

The new Harvard Business School Corporate Training and Development Catalog is created exclusively for those who design and develop custom training programs.

It's filled cover-to-cover with valuable materials you can put to work on the spot. You'll find a comprehensive selection of cases, *Harvard Business Review* articles, videos, Special Collections, books, and more.

Our new catalog covers the critical management topics affecting corporations today, like Leadership, Quality, Global Business, Marketing, and Strategy, to name a few. And it's all organized, indexed, and cross-referenced to make it easy for you to find precisely what you need.

Harvard Business School Publishing

HOW TO ORDER

To order by FAX, dial 617-495-6985. Or call 617-495-6192. Please mention telephone order code 132A. Or send a check for $10 payable to HBS Publishing Division, or credit card information to: HBS Corporate Training and Development Catalog, Harvard Business School Publishing Division, Operations Department, Boston, MA 02163. **All orders must be prepaid.**

Order No.	Title	Qty. ×	Price +	Shipping* =	Total
39001	Catalog		$10		

*U.S. and Canada: 5% for UPS or first class mail. *Foreign Surface Mail:* 15% for parcel post registered; allow 3–6 mos. *Express Deliveries (credit card orders only):* billed at cost; all foreign orders not designating express delivery will be sent by registered surface mail.

☐ Check enclosed (in U.S. funds drawn on U.S. bank)

☐ VISA   ☐ American Express   ☐ MasterCard

Card Number_____ Exp. Date_____

Signature_____

Telephone_____ FAX_____

Name_____

Organization_____

Street_____

City_____ State/Zip_____

Country_____ ☐ Home Address ☐ Organization Address

Please Reference Telephone Order Source Code 132A